New Life in Christ
by Faith

Mary J. Bryant

"I do declare that I am no longer under condemnation because I am in Christ Jesus. And because I am in Christ Jesus I walk after the Spirit and not after the flesh. I am empowered and strengthen to do this because the law of the Spirit of life in Christ Jesus has made me free from the law of sin and death."

Romans 8:1-2

Kingdom Builders Publications LLC

© 2017 by Mary J. Bryant
Kingdom Builders Publications

All rights reserved. No part of this book may be reproduced or transmitted in any form or by any means without written permission from the author.

Library of Congress Control Number: 2017958932
Soft Cover ISBN: 9780692975282
Hard Cover Limited Special Edition: 9780692975268

Edited by Michael Bryant
Kingdom Builders Publications

Cover Design LoMar Designs

Permission and Copyright Information
God's Word Translation (GW): Scripture is taken from GOD'S WORD®, © 1995 God's Word to the Nations. Used by permission of Baker Publishing Group.
Scripture quotations marked TPT are taken from John: Eternal Love, The Passion
Translation®, copyright © 2014, 2015. Used by permission of Broad Street
Publishing Group, LLC, Racine, Wisconsin, USA. All rights reserved.
Scripture quotations marked (NLT) are taken from the Holy Bible, New Living Translation, copyright © 1996, 2004, 2007 by Tyndale House Foundation. Used by permission of Tyndale House Publishers, Inc., Carol Stream, Illinois 60188. All rights reserved.
"Scripture quotations taken from the Amplified® Bible (AMP), Copyright © 2015 by The Lockman Foundation
Used by permission. www.Lockman.org"
All other scriptures are taken from the King James Version

New Life in Christ

This Book Belongs to

DEDICATION

This book is dedicated to God the Father, God the Son, and God the Holy Spirit. I give all glory, praise, and honor to God. I am so thankful for the grace given to me to be able to write and publish such an important message. I am truly humbled for the opportunity. Apostle Paul wrote that "It's not important who does the planting, or who does the watering. What's important is that God makes the seed grow."

(1 Corinthians 3:7 NLT).

	Dedication	v
	Acknowledgments	1
	Prayer	2
	Foreword	3
	Introduction	4
	Prologue	8
1	Transition: From Kingdom of Darkness to Kingdom of Light	10
2	Dedication and Commitment	17
3	Endurance	19
4	The Blood Never Loses its Power	25
5	New Life in Christ by Faith	32
6	New Identity in Christ	44
7	The Church of God in Christ Jesus	49
8	The Marks of a Sheep	57
9	God's Amazing Grace	60
10	Grace the Power to Succeed	70
11	Growing Spiritually in the New Life	76
12	New Beginning: The Promise of the Holy Spirit	86
13	Assurance of Salvation – A Prepared Place for a Prepared People	95
14	Our Goal: Christ Formed in Us	100
	Epilogue	104
	How to experience New Life in Christ	107
	About the Author	110

ACKNOWLEDGMENTS

To Michael Bryant, Sr., my loving husband, who has been with me on this journey from the beginning, thanks for all your support and encouragement, and for completing the edits for the book. I love you Dear, and our wonderful family: Michael, Megan, Marquis (our three wonderful children), and Michaela (our adorable granddaughter).

To Shirley Ford, (who affectionately calls me her Sunshine) for her zeal and zest in promoting the sales of all of my books, thank you.

To Louise W. Rouse, Pastor and Apostle of Rehoboth Restoration Church, thank you Sissy for all your prayers and support.

To Dr. Gerald Seals, Pastor of Living Word Church and fellowship, for his prayers and willingness to assist with editing the first draft of the manuscript, thank you.

To Dr. Blakely N. Scott, Pastor of First Nazareth Baptist Church, for so graciously providing the forward for this book. Words of gratitude are inadequate. Thank you.

To my wonderful Family and friends.

To my publisher, Louise Smith, here we go again... Thanks to all of you for your continued support, prayers, and encouragement on this publishing journey.

Let God be Glorified.

Prayer

Our Father, thank You for the new life we have in Christ because of the measure of faith you have given each of us. I pray that we will be filled with the knowledge of Your will in wisdom and spiritual understanding, and that we may walk worthy of the Lord unto all pleasing, being fruitful in every good work, and increasing in the knowledge of God. I pray that we will be strengthened with all might, according to Your glorious power, unto all patience and longsuffering with joyfulness.

Father, help Christ to be formed in us. Help us to labor so that Christ may be formed in all the church. Help us be about our Father's business, seeking His will, seeking Him. Let us be changed for his purpose.

I also pray that You have made us to be partakers of the inheritance of the saints in light. Thank You that You have delivered us from the power of darkness and translated us into the Kingdom of Your Son, Jesus, because in Him we have redemption through His blood, even the forgiveness of sins.

It is my prayer Father that we continue in the faith grounded and settled and be not move away from the hope of the gospel for us that endures to the end shall be saved (Matthew 10:22).

Thank You Father for another opportunity to be obedient to Your will. All praise, glory, and honor be to You. In the Lord's name, I do pray. Amen and thank You Jesus.

Foreword

I thank God for giving me the rich privilege to peruse the pages of this special document on what it means to be in fellowship with Him Who has been so kind and generous to extend the opportunity to anyone and everyone. The thought provoking, spirit lifting and conscious convicting outlay of sacred scripture in combination with insightful commentary in this book is going to certainly be a blessing to the Body of Christ. Very often, we have a tendency to become so involved in doing Kingdom work, that if we are not careful, we could lose sight of how important it is to maintain the upkeep on our own relationship as well as to be available to assist others in their quest to walk with the Savior in a committed faith relationship.

We owe a debt of gratitude to Minister Mary Bryant for this powerful undertaking and for her passion for the cause as it is appropriately tempered by her compassion for her fellow compatriots in the faith. With sensitivity to the desires of those who aim to be genuine Christian and without being so rigid and fundamental in her approach, she gives a well-balanced presentation that should be palatable to all who are earnestly seeking to stabilize their status as twice born persons.

I urge you as you view the pages of this book that you view it through the lens of hopeful expectation for victory for all of those who come to Jesus Christ as their personal Savior and Lord. Hopefully, the excitement will be maintained and the appreciation for what the Lord has done through His finished work on Calvary will stay at a constant and consistent level.

Prepare to be blessed,

Blakely N. Scott
Pastor, First Nazareth Baptist Church

Introduction

New Life: Based on Christ's Death: "But now he has reconciled you by his physical body through death, to present you before God as a people who are holy, faultless, and without blame." (Colossians 1:22, CEB)

New Life: Received by faith: "For by grace are ye saved through faith; and that not of yourselves: it is the gift of God:" (Ephesians 2:8, KJV)

New Life: A free Gift: "The wages that sin pays are death, but God's gift is eternal life in Christ Jesus our Lord." (Romans 6:23, CEB)

New life in Christ means we have a new nature, which refers to the spiritual transformation that happens within the inner being when a person believes in Christ as Savior. Our new life in Christ begins by faith. When we are born-again by the Spirit of God, we become new creatures or new creations. We no longer walk in the futility of our mind which was darkened in our understanding because of the hardness of heart (*Ephesians 4:17-18*). We, therefore put aside the old self or old nature and be renewed in the spirit of our minds and put on the new self or new nature, which is the likeness of God (*Ephesians 4:22-24*). In other words, we turn away from our old way of thinking and the lusts of our flesh turning to God's way and walking in the light of His Kingdom. We are to forsake all (repent or turn away) and turn to God for our salvation. We are rescued and delivered from the penalty of sin (death, separation from God) and from the power of sin.

The suffering, the death, the burial, and the resurrection of Jesus were for redemption into a new life. We were not redeemed to stay in an infantile state for the enemy to continue to deceive us. Because of the Sovereignty (His divine power) of God, we have been given every all things that pertain to life and godliness *(2 Peter 1:3)*. Therefore, it is up to us to give all diligence and add to the faith *(2 Peter 5-11)*. God came to redeem us but it is our responsibility to grow in grace and to allow the Spirit of God to sanctify us continually.

The revelation of how Christ rescued us from destruction and God's wrath should be enough to motivate us to learn as much as He allows us to know about Him. The Bible confirms that they who hunger and thirst after righteousness shall be fed *(Matthew 5:6)*. In *Matthew 6:33*, we are instructed to seek the kingdom and His righteousness first.

As a new creation in Christ, we need a lot more of Jesus and a lot less of ourselves. I have gotten to the place in my relationship with Jesus that I say: I decrease so that He can increase; Less of me and more of Him; None of me and all of Him. It should be our desire to be more like Jesus since we were originally made in "Their" (Let Us – *Genesis 1:26*) image and likeness. We have to have the mind of Christ [Let this mind be in me that is also in Christ Jesus –Philippians 2:5]. *Romans 12:2* states, "Do not conform to the pattern of this world, but be transformed by the renewing of your mind." (NIV).

Jesus came to change us and fashion us for Kingdom life right here on earth to prepare us for eternal life with Him. Jesus came in the sinful image of humanity. He was betrayed by a sinner and arrested by sinners. He suffered and died for sinners and was resurrected to justify sinners. Now, He is seated at the right hand of God to keep us, sanctify us, and sustain us. Through our Lord and Savior, we have been given grace to succeed in this new life. Once we are converted and regenerated, Christ becomes our life (*Galatians 2:20, Romans 8:10, Colossians 3:4, Philippians 1:21*). We become united with Christ and we are one with Him in Spirit (*1 Corinthians 6:17*).

The challenge to walk upright before the Lord may seem difficult and unreachable, but God does not leave us to walk this journey alone. Throughout the Bible, God offers the assurance and reassurance that He will never leave us nor forsake us *(Isaiah 41:10; Matthew 28:20)*. Therefore, as new creatures, we must learn to walk with God, not in opposition to Him, but in agreement with His plan, His purpose, and His will. We agree with Him (*Amos 3:3*).

The new life cannot and will not be successful apart from Christ. Our lives would be fruitless and unproductive (John 15:5). There has to be revelation that the Good News of the Kingdom of God is not only facts to believe, but it is also the life we shall live: A life of righteousness appropriate for the person justified freely by God's grace through the redemption that is in Christ Jesus (*Romans 3:24*).

Receiving Jesus Christ as Lord and Savior is the wisest decision we will ever make. Now let's deny ourselves, take up our cross, and follow Jesus (*Luke 9:23)*. It is my aim to make more Christians aware of their position in Christ and to motivate them to draw upon their spiritual resource in their daily lives.

This book is just the appetizer to the main course which is the Bible, the Word of God. I encourage you to study the scriptures and let it renew your mind and mature you in the grace and knowledge of God in your new life in Christ. You will gain valuable knowledge and wisdom of how to live this new life on earth. You will become a true witness of Jesus Christ, our Lord and Savior. It is my hope and prayer that we all be more aware of our position in Christ. Our practice must represent our position and our position must represent our practice. The Bible teaches us to "walk worthy of the vocation wherewith ye are called" (*Ephesians 4:1; 1 Thessalonians 2:12*). "For we are his workmanship, created in Christ Jesus unto good works, which God hath before ordained (prepared) that we should walk in them" (Ephesians 2:10).

Prologue

When I first began this journey to become a published author, I was hesitant, doubtful, and discouraged. Fear tried to keep me from proceeding, but I pressed on by grace and by believing the Lord was leading and guiding me. So, in December 2013, I published my first book, **Prayers, Poems, and Precious Moment**. I give God the glory. My second book, **I Recommend Jesus**, was like roaring waters inside of me to write. Once again, I felt apprehensive but excited that God was using me for His glory by way of this book. I was a little bit stronger and courageous in my writing experience. I had matured over the two years because of the grace of God.

I now present this third book, **New Life in Christ by Faith**, a follow up of **I Recommend Jesus**, if you don't have this book yet, please secure your copy today. I felt compelled to write what has been ignited in me. I walk by faith, not by sight, believing the Lord will supply everything I need for this journey.

It is my belief that there has to be foundational teaching of Apostolic Doctrine when a person is born again into the new life. We are told that Jesus has died for our sins, but then what? As a newly converted disciple of Christ, you have to desire the sincere milk of the word that you may grow up in your salvation (*1 Peter 2:2*). This is not just a once or twice a week undertaking for 30 minutes to an hour. The mind has to be renewed to grow spiritually. Without the renewing of the mind, there will be no transformation. As a follower of Christ, we are to grow in the grace and knowledge of Jesus Christ, our Lord and Savior (*2 Peter 3:18*).

It is **not** my purpose to "beat" anyone up or "condemn" with this book, but it is my earnest desire that as the body of Christ, we mature in the knowledge and understanding of our Lord and Savior. A babe in Christ is still carnal minded and operates by the flesh. Apostle Paul wrote to the Corinthians about this same matter. He wrote in *1 Corinthians 3:1*, "Brothers and sisters, I could not address you as people who live by the Spirit but as people who are still worldly--mere infants in Christ." (NIV). Spiritual maturity keeps us from being ineffective and unproductive (*1 Peter 1:1-12*).

Transition: From the Kingdom of Darkness to the Kingdom of Light

Off with the Old and on with the New

Chapter One

The old man is still present in the new life (*Ephesians 4:22; Colossians 3:9*). In order for the new man to be visible we must take off the old man and put on the new man (*Colossians 3:10*). In other words, the new nature has to be cultivated or nurtured by spiritual transition with spiritual decisiveness to grow in Christ. Being a born-again believer, we can't live any kind of way before the Lord. There has to be the act of turning away from the old mind set and now living unto God. The Bible is our instructions on how the new man lives and looks after being converted. There has to be a conviction in the heart to live this new life by faith, for without faith it is impossible to please God. When the word is preached, it has to be mixed with faith (*Hebrews 4:2; Romans 10:17*). We have the message of supreme hope in that the Spirit of God can accomplish a life-changing transformation for all who will only believe in Christ.

The transition from darkness to light has the most awesome requirements of God. That is, we must be conformed to His ethical and moral standards (*Psalm 15:2; Micah 6:8*). Let me explain. Since God is holy He cannot allow sinners into His presence (*Isaiah 6:3-5*). Therefore, He sent

Christ to earth so that He can deliver us from darkness into the Light. In other words, God, at the cross, treated Christ as though He had committed our sins even though He was righteous. But when we believe in Christ, God treats us as though we were as righteous as Christ (*Ephesians 2:8-9*).

There has to be a distinction between the world and the Church of Jesus Christ. As born-again believers, we must stand firm in the word of God. God's Word never teaches disciples to blend in with the world and compromise the truth. These are those who profess that they know God, in their works they deny Him (*Titus 1:16*). Titus teaches us that we should deny ungodliness and worldly lusts, live soberly, righteously, and godly in this world (*Titus 2:12*). When we were transitioned, we were made right with God. We have been given the robe of righteousness and the garments of salvation *(Isaiah 61:10)*.

Those who have been rescued and redeemed from the domain of darkness and transferred into the Kingdom of the Son of love (*Colossians 1:13*) has been placed in God's family. Though we are all God's offspring in that He is our Creator *(Acts 17:28-29)*, we are not all His children. For a sinful person to become a child of God, miraculous transformation must take place. Once we are born again by faith we are made new and now in the family of God. We now can call ourselves Christians. The term Christian was given to the early church by unbelievers in Antioch (*Acts 11:26*). Because they belonged to Christ; it was probably intended to be a derogatory term. Jesus never called His followers Christians, but Christians are people who have placed their faith in Him

(John 1:12). A true Christian is more than one in name only. A true Christian is also a disciple of Christ. Jesus calls us to deny ourselves, take up our cross, and follow Him daily. There is a cost in being a disciple of Christ; we have counted up the cost and committed our lives completely to Christ. Becoming a disciple is a call to sacrifice and follow wherever Jesus, our Lord, leads us. A disciple lives by the teachings of Jesus and makes Him the number one priority. A disciple is also actively involved in making other disciples *(Matthew 28:19-20)*. Apostle Paul puts it this way: "I have been crucified with Christ and I no longer live, but Christ lives in me. The life I live in the body, I live by faith in the Son of God, who loved me and gave himself for me." *(Galatians 2:20)*

So, why do some still live as they choose? I often hear statements that "we all still sin every day", "we are human", or we are not perfect". God never told us to be perfect in our own perfection, but it is in Christ that we are complete and made perfect. The Bible teaches me that we are to be no longer slaves to sin, but to righteousness. John wrote that if we walk in the light we cannot sin. Now I know God is faithful and just to forgive us of our sin if we confess it, but that doesn't mean we sin every day or sin continually. We must turn to God in repentance and have faith in Christ Jesus *(Acts 20:21)*. Therefore, Christians who are disciples should have a lifestyle that is clearly different from those of the world. Apostle Paul wrote this to the Ephesians:

> *And you hath he quickened, who were dead in trespasses and sins; wherein in time past ye walked according to the course of this world,*

> *according to the prince of the power of the air, the spirit that now worketh in the children of disobedience: Among whom also we all had our conversation in times past in the lust of our flesh, fulfilling the desires of the flesh and of the mind; and were by nature the children of wrath, ever as others. (Ephesians 2:1-3)*

When we are born again, there has been a "quickening". We were made alive. We had to be quickened because we were "dead in trespasses and sins" according to *Ephesians 2:1*. The new life means there has been a spiritual transformation. The old life now has been brought under subjection, and the new life now must be purposefully cultivated or nurtured by spiritual decisiveness to grow in the grace and knowledge of Christ *(2 Peter 3:18)* because He has brought out of darkness into His marvelous light *(1 Peter 2:9)*. The message of the new life is a message of supreme hope because the Holy Spirit can accomplish a life-changing transformation. Our walk, now, is considered to be worthy of God's calling *(Ephesians 4:1-32)* wherein we forsake uncleanness and unfruitfulness (*Ephesians 5:1-14*) by the power of the Holy Spirit *(Ephesians 5:15-6:22)*.

We must remember that there are certain principles that we have to walk by. We cannot walk with God by our own principles and plans. God is working to bring us into conformity with Jesus Christ. As born-again believers, we were buried with Christ and raised with Him to walk in the newness of life (*Romans 6:4*). God gives us the power to resist and overcome sin. James teaches to submit to God, and resist the devil (*4:7*). Because Christ has overcome Satan and the world, we, who are in Christ, have the same power to be overcomers.

> *1 John 3:5-6, "And ye know that he was manifested to take way our sins; and in Him is no sin. Whosoever abideth in him sinneth not: whosoever sinneth hath not seen him neither know him. Little children, let no man deceive you: he that doeth righteousness is righteous, even as he is righteous. He that committeth sin is of the devil; for the devil sinneth from the beginning. For this purpose the Son of God was manifested, that he might destroy the works of the devil."*

My point is that we don't have to continue to be in bondage to sin if we don't want to be. When we remain in Christ, we cannot continuously sin. It is never necessary for us to sin *(1 John 2:1)*. We must believe the Word of God.

So, if we fall, confess and know that He is faithful and just to forgive and cleanse from all unrighteousness *(1 John 1:9)*. We should never attempt to excuse or condone our sin; however, there is no sin too great or no sin too small because the efficacious Blood of Christ is able to cleanse us from all unrighteousness. Sin is to be confessed and forsaken as we yield our bodies completely to God so that fellowship will be restored with Him. The new life is not to work our way into heaven or even work to be saved. Salvation is a gift and ultimately rests on God's faithfulness and grace, not on one's perfect work. The good work we have been created do is because we have a new life in Christ.

John 8:12 teaches us that Jesus is the light of the world and if we follow Him, we will not walk in darkness. So, there can be victory for us when we follow Jesus. He is our Righteous Advocate before the Father (*1 John 1:5-2:22*) and His blood continually cleanses us from all sin. No one is without sin before receiving salvation and forgiveness and justification, but thanks be to God we have been justified through the blood of Christ. As Jesus told the woman caught in adultery, "go and sin no more" *(John 8:11)*. I do believe the Lord expects us not to sin no more through the help He has given us by the Holy Spirit.

Although the Lord is not slack concerning His promise, He is longsuffering and that longsuffering is salvation for He doesn't want anyone to perish but come to repentance (turn away from darkness and turn to the light). However, the day of the Lord will be like a thief that comes in the night. That is why Jesus exhorts the disciples. Therefore, we must grow in grace and not fall from our steadfastness *(2 Peter 3:9-18)*. Jesus told His disciples to watch and pray that they enter into temptation: the spirit is indeed wiling, but the flesh is weak *(Matthew 28:41)*. Only those who are in the light will not be caught off guard when He returns.

Though temptations come, if we abide in Christ we can have confidence and assurance before Him. Our confidence is that our sins are forgiven and we can enjoy fellowship with God through Jesus Christ. Because He is able to keep us from falling and present us faultless before God *(Jude 24)*. Being transformed into the likeness of Christ makes us incompatible with sin because sin is contrary to the person and work of Christ *(1 John 3:4-6)*. Our behavior of fellowship with God should reflect that we are abiding in Christ. That is insofar as we do so abide, we do not sin. So, saints of God, we can be certain that sin is a threat to fellowship and it should be regarded as foreign to our position in Christ *(1 John 5:18; Romans 6)*. Because the Lord himself knows how to deliver the godly out any and all temptations *(2 Peter 2:9)*. He is faithful to provide a way of escape out so we can endure it *(1 Corinthians 13:10)*. Now that is reassuring to know. There has to be practice with professing. Because profession without practice is useless.

God has equipped you and I for a holy walk or holy way of living, but the choice is ours to make. After we have received the gift of salvation by believing and putting our faith in Jesus Christ and Him alone, we are to present ourselves to God as living sacrifices, totally committed; totally surrendered. This is the transition we have to make from the old nature to the new nature.

Dedication and Commitment

Chapter Two

I believe the first two steps in living the new life in Christ by faith are dedication and commitment. We first dedicate our body as a living sacrifice to God. We must also avoid conforming to world because we are called out of it and to the obedience that comes from faith and the calling to belong to Christ (*Romans 1:5-6*). We must strive to be transformed by the Word of God; in doing this, we can discover God's perfect will for our lives (*Romans 12:1-2*). After we have dedicated our bodies, we then commit our salvation to God (*2 Timothy 1:12*). We also commit our works and ways to God (*Proverbs 16:37*). We commit our goals to God (*John 5:8; Psalm 37:5*). Our agenda becomes God's agenda.

God expects us to worship Him, and we must understand that every aspect of our life is spiritual. Everything we do can be a way of worshipping Him. The way we live our lives is the highest form of manifested praise to God; therefore, the character of our lives must be shaped by our dedication to Christ (*Hebrews 13:1-9*).

When our hearts are pure, the rest of our lives will also be pure. We will clothe ourselves with humility, not only in our actions, but also in our thoughts. Our speech will show our contentment as well-felt in our inner desires. Our compassion will be godly in deed and in the motives behind the acts. In other words, out of a pure heart comes a holy life.

Though this may be a challenge, it is still in our reach by the grace given to us through Jesus Christ *(John 1:17)*. Apostle Paul recorded in *2 Corinthians 12:9* that God's grace is sufficient in our weakness. We should not trust in ourselves, but in God *(2 Corinthians 1:9)*. It is vital, as a child of God, to commit everything to Him even when we suffer *(1 Peter 4:19)*. We can rejoice in our commitment because it will be accepted and honored by the Lord *(1 Corinthians 15:58)*. Proverbs 16:3 tells us that when we commit our works unto the Lord, our thoughts shall be established, and when our ways please Him, our enemies will be made peaceful towards us *(Proverbs 16:7)*. It truly is a win-win situation. We must not let the world around us squeeze us into its mold, but allow God, our Creator, to re-mold our minds from within, so that we may prove in practice that the plan of God for us is good. It meets all of His demands and moves us toward the goal of true maturity *(Romans 12:12)*.

The Bible teaches us that the saints of God reflect like mirrors the glory of the Lord, and we are transformed by the Spirit of the Lord in ever-increasing splendor into His own image *(2 Corinthians 3:18)*. Don't you want to be like Jesus? Let's show the world to whom we belong.

Endurance

Chapter Three

"For you have need of endurance, so that when you have done the will of God you may receive what is promised." ~Hebrews 10:36 ESV

"The goal of our faith is salvation of our souls-now that you are receiving the goal of your faith, the salvation of your souls." ~ 1 Peter 1:9 Berean Study Bible

Baker's Evangelical Dictionary of Biblical Theology defines endurance as continuing Christian commitment in the face of difficulty; I like to say it is pressing our way through that which we don't have the ability or strength in and of ourselves. Endurance is struggling not to give up and having faith in God despite the many trials or tests that come our way as Christians. Apostle Paul wrote to Timothy that all who want to live godly lives in Christ Jesus will go through challenging situations *(2 Timothy 3:12-13)*. Jesus Himself told His disciples that they would have tribulations *(John 16:33)*. Christ is the perfect example of endurance. He endured the shame, suffering, and a death He didn't deserve *(Hebrews 12:2; Hebrews 9:11-14)*. He became the propitiation for our sins and those of the whole world *(1 John 2:2; Romans 3:25)*. Some might say, "…but that was Jesus Christ, the Savior of the world," well, look at the book of *Hebrews, Chapter 11*. The writer illustrates the faith of a group of people who endured trials by faith because of the promises and purposes of God *(Hebrews 12:11)*.

I believe endurance is a Christ-like quality God wants to

develop in His children's lives as a part of spiritual growth and maturity *(2 Thessalonians 3:5)*. James also encourages believers about trials and testing of our faith. He explains that it is good to go through trials and tests because doing so produces endurance *(James 1:2-4)*. Friedrich Nietzsche wrote, "That which does not kill us makes us stronger." If we allow the trials, tribulations, and trials we experience to shape our character, we will mature in our Christian walk and faith. These sufferings produce endurance, endurance produces character, and character produces hope *(Romans 5:3-4)*. We know that our hope is anchored in Jesus Christ (Psalm 39:7), and our hope in Jesus does not disappoint or makes us ashamed *(Romans 5:5)*.

We can endure through our knowledge of God's will. In Colossians, chapter one, Paul prays for the fruitful growth of the Christians at Colossae. Our growth in the wisdom and understanding of who we are in Christ gives us the necessary patience and endurance to be steadfast in whatever trials we face. We are to pursue endurance along with righteousness, godliness, faithfulness, love, and gentleness *(1 Timothy 6:11-12)*. We get power to endure from God Himself. "Being strengthened with all power according to his glorious might so that you may have great endurance and patience" *(Colossians 1:11)*.

Endurance is something we develop day-by-day and even moment-by-moment. It is the truest expression or manifestation of God's grace. As Jesus told Paul, "My grace is sufficient." *James 5:11* states, "As you know, we count as blessed those who have preserved. You have heard of Job's perseverance and have seen what the Lord finally brought about. The Lord is full of compassion and mercy." Our compassionate and merciful God shows His love and favor to those who endure trials and afflictions to His glory.

We have to be steadfast as we endure. Endurance requires a commitment of time; that time commitment means spending more time with God, our source. We must spend time in His Word and in prayer. We have to connect with God to let Him pour into us to refresh and strengthen us. Jesus always made it a priority to be alone with the Father *(Mark 1:35, Matthew 14:23, Luke 22:32)*. *Isaiah 40:31* states that "But those who wait for the Lord will find new strength *(NLT)*." The Lord is faithful in keeping His Word *(Psalm 89:33)*. We don't have to endure on our own because the Lord helps us. It is important that we endure until the end. *Matthew 24:13* states, "But he that shall endure unto the end, the same shall be saved" *(KJV)*. Endurance gives us assurance of salvation. *Jude, verse 3* exhorts us to "contend for the faith," and when we endure, that is what we are doing.

I believe transformation plays a big part in our endurance. Notice I did not say evolution; there is a big difference in the two. To be transformed is different from evolution because the former has a defined goal. Evolution is defined as "the process by which different kinds of living organisms are thought to have developed and diversified from earlier forms during the history of the earth" (Prezi.com) To be transformed comes from the Greek word metamorphoo, from which we get the English word metamorphosis, which means "a change of the form or nature of a thing or person into a completely different one by natural or supernatural means (*Bibles for America*)." Christ's meaning of transformation is the revealing of His character in each life, and the goal is to reinstate His creation back into its original intent. Each of us should ask the question: Is Christianity just a spiritual security blanket, or is it a truth that radically transforms us in the way we live our lives? Do we vacillate or waver between worldly values and Christian values? *Acts 26:19* states, "That they should repent, turn to God and do works befitting repentance."

I once read that the Christian life is not a 100-yard dash, but a marathon. Another way to say this is: I don't want to have a microwave faith but a slow cooker faith. Because of trials and hardships, we have to be faithful even when we don't want to be. Apostle Paul wrote to Timothy in *2 Timothy 2:8-13*, endure hardship because Christ has risen and His Word is powerful and His promises are trustworthy. The Apostle is encouraging Timothy to embrace hardship for the sake of the gospel (*1:8; 2:3*). Though we are sometimes under pressure to comprise the Gospel, we must fight against it. God promises that He will keep all whom He saves, but the process is not automatic. We must take an active role by being faithful. The suffering for the gospel now will result in eternal glory, and if we want to endure this marathon, we have to stand firm through the pressures, and even persecution, to testify like Apostle Paul as a personal witness. God saved me from my sins by His pure abounding grace through Christ Jesus. "Remember that Jesus Christ of the seed of David was raised from the dead according to my gospel" (*2 Timothy 28*). Through Christ we have been reconciled to God and united to Him. Through that union with Him we might be made righteous *(2 Corinthians 5:19-21)*.

In Hebrews, Chapter 12, Jesus Christ has given us the best example of endurance. He was flesh and blood and "made like unto his brethren" in all things *(Hebrews 2:17)* to bring "many sons to glory" *(Hebrews 2:10)*. Jesus was tempted just like we are, but was yet without sin *(4:15)*. Jesus endured great hostility though he was innocent of the crime they accused Him of; He was slapped, mocked, taunted, spat on, His beard was pulled out, flogged, scourged, stripped naked, and a thorny crown was placed on His head. He was severely beaten with a whip or lash made of leather thongs which contained metal fragments and pieces of bones that literally ripped into His flesh. He was crucified; crucifixion is said to be the worst kind of death - especially if you are innocent. Though many do not know Jesus was completely naked on the cross, nailed hand and foot to it by nails that looked like railroad spikes. When the Bible refers to His "hands," it means His wrists because they were considered to be part of the hands. One spike was used for His feet, and His knees were bent. Jesus had to painfully push Himself up to breathe. He hung on that cross for some six hours in utter agony after being tortured all night long. Now that is love. "Greater love hath no man than this, that a man lay done his life for his friends" *(John 15:13)*. He chose to be a ransom for many. "No man taketh it from me, but I lay it down of myself. I have power to lay it down and I have power to take it again" *(John 10:18)*. Jesus willingly endured the shame and disgrace of the cross for our redemption. He took our place.

It is with patient endurance we can run the race set before us (*12:1*), not as dash, but as a marathon. We can run this race by the great cloud of witness that surrounds us as we look to Jesus Christ, the author and finisher or our faith (*12:2*). He could endure the cross because He knew the joy that was set before Him. *Psalm 68:18* states, "You have ascended on high, You have led away captive Your captives; You have received gifts among men, even from the rebellious also, that the LORD God may dwell there" (AMP). He knew Golgotha was just before the glory. He knew that His life was beyond the cross because He would be seated at the right hand of the Father. He knew that He was going to set many captives free to receive His glorious church. What an example! He has the power to help us to endure until the end.

The Blood Never Loses its Power

Chapter Four

The Blood of Jesus has made all nations of men that dwell on the earth (*Acts 17:26*), because we are all descendants of the first man and woman. We all are descendants of the first Adam and born with the sin nature. Therefore, all human beings need to repent and receive the free gift of salvation. Because of the Blood of Jesus, all who believe in Him can be saved. The one Blood created all, and the one Blood saves all. Christ's Blood is the cure for the depraved state we inherited from Adam. The Book of Leviticus shadows the Blood as "the life Blood," and through the Cross, Christ secured our salvation and the deliverance from the guilt, shame, and power of death. You could say that the Blood of Jesus gives us a blood transfusion, and our DNA is changed - made new. The same Blood makes peace between God and man. Christ Blood is efficacious in cleansing past sins, present sins, all possible sins, the power of sin, and the penalty of sin.

I truly believe the Blood of Christ is the most precious and priceless gift God has given to His human creation. I seek revelation to fully understand its value, virtue, and power. We often sing about the power of the Blood. "The Blood will never lose its Power." "There is Power, Power, wondering working Power in the Precious Blood of the Lamb." "What can wash away my sins? Nothing but the Blood of Jesus." "I'm saved, washed, cleansed, Blood-washed." We sing these songs with such joy and conviction, but how many really enter into the Power of the Blood? What does the Power of the Blood means? So, again, yes, "without the shedding of Blood there would be no remission or forgiveness of sin" (*Hebrews 9:22*). The Blood frees us from the bondage of iniquity (*Romans 8:2*). The Blood covers and cleanses all our sins *(1 John 1:7)*. Even more than that, the Blood can manifest wonderful changes in our life.

Genesis records the first sacrifice needed for the atonement of sin. Adam and Eve made themselves aprons from fig leaves to cover themselves, but that covering was not suitable in God's eyes. God, took an innocent animal and killed it to make a proper covering of atonement for their sin (*Genesis 3*). The blood of that innocent animal was shed to cover them, thus, becoming the beginning of the scarlet thread of redemption. (*Genesis 3:21*). Then in Exodus, the Passover is the foreshadow of the saving Blood of the Lamb of God. In chapter 12, the LORD told Moses and Aaron to use a branch of hyssop, dip it in the blood of a slain lamb, and sprinkle it on the lintel and two side-posts of their front door *(Exodus 12:22)*. When the Blood was sprinkled on the door posts and the lintel of the front door, the death angel passed over the house. This was salvation through the blood and again the scarlet thread of redemption. "And it came to pass the selfsame day that the LORD did bring the children of Israel out of the land of Egypt by their armies *(vs. 51, KJV)*. Revelation: The Blood brings us all the way out. After the redemption, comes the sanctifying; but to be sanctified, God has to do the leading (*Exodus 13:17-22)*. As people who have received redemption, they must now be set apart to walk with God.

The Blood that was shed on Calvary. The Blood that never lose its Power – "it flows to the lowest valley and flows to the highest mountain. No sin is out of the reach of the Blood Cleansing Power. The song says "There is a fountain filled with Blood with Blood drawn from Emmanuel's vein, and sinners plunged beneath that flow lose all their guilt and stain … *(Matthew 26:28 ESV, Zechariah 13:1; John 1:29; Ephesians 1:7)*. The fountain that flows from Emmanuel's veins represents the death of Christ Jesus, the crown of thrones on His head *(John 19:2)*, the flogging *(John 19:1)*, the nails in His hands and feet *(Matthew 27:35)*, the piercing of His side, and the Blood and water that flowed out as a symbol of redemption *(John 19:34)*. Because of the mercy and grace of Christ, salvation is the fruit/gift that comes from repentance and the forgiveness of sins by His Precious Blood *(Ephesians 1:7)*. This is a continual running fountain that cleanses us from all righteousness *(1 John 1:7)*. "Thy Precious Blood shall never lose its power … Be saved, to sin no more, be saved to sin no more" – the song lyrics says: This is the power of the sanctifying redeeming Blood of Christ. We don't have to continually sin. Jesus told the woman caught in adultery in to go and sin no more *(John 8:11)*. I don't believe we should habitually sin once we have "applied the Blood". No, I am not talking about being "perfect", but being transformed into the new life in Christ under the Blood. We have to rely on the power of the Blood to leave the life of sin because we have inherited the nature to sin at any moment. However, we don't have to. It is the sanctification process that we must allow to take place in our lives. Despite the pain, shame, and suffering it cost Jesus, to secure our redemption and pardon, He offers it free to you and I. Christ paid it all and we are freely forgiven and have power not to sin. All done by the "riches of God's grace" (*Ephesians 1:7*). Sin doesn't overcome the Blood but it is the Blood that overcomes sin.

"I beseech you therefore, brethren, by the mercies of God, that ye present your bodies a living sacrifice, holy, acceptable unto God, which is your reasonable service. And be not conformed to this world: but be ye transformed to this world: but be ye transformed by the renewing of your mind, that ye may prove what is that good, and acceptable, and perfect, will of God (*Romans 12:1-2 KJV*). We have to be yielded and surrendered vessels/instruments for God's service in both the body and the mind (*Romans 12:1; 1 Corinthians 6:20, Romans 12:2*). To believe requires both knowledge (renewing the mind) and volition (the choice to change). It is with the body the actions conceived in the mind are manifested. *James 1:15* states, "Then, after desire has conceived, it gives birth to sin; and sin, when it is full grown, gives birth to death (NIV). The desire conceived in the mind is carried out/birthed in the body. Please note that the transformation Paul wrote about is a lifelong process that will be completed until we are with Christ (*Philippians 1:6; 1 John 3:2*). No, we are not "perfect" in and of ourselves, but we are perfect in Christ. "Whom we preach, warning every man, and teaching every man in all wisdom; that we may present every man perfect in Christ Jesus (*Colossians 1:28*). I encourage you to let Christ be formed in you (*Galatians 4:19*).

As the New Testament Church, we partake in Communion regularly. I wonder if we "drink the cup unworthily." Is it done out of tradition? Do we discern Christ's body properly? Do we know that it is one Jesus but two bodies (the body given and the body raised)? Do we partake of the Lord's Table, symbolic of the body given for us not broken (none of His bones were broken -*John 19:36)* for us and the Blood shed for the remission of sin, yet not believing the Power of the Blood? Isn't this having a form of godliness but denying the power of it *(2 Timothy 3:5)*? We have to believe in the total victory of Christ's Blood. I know you may be saying: "I am not there yet;" "I am human;" or "I still struggle," but the truest evidence of faith is rest. We can say and believe: Because of the Blood of Christ, I am saved, I am being saved I will be saved, I am healed. The Blood allows us to stand before a holy God. Scripture asks the question: How will stand before the God *(Psalm 24:3)*. Yes, we are required to live a life of righteousness by faith in God *(Romans 1:17)*. Therefore, I encourage all of us to make sure that we live a life of faith in God that produces a life of righteousness for the just shall live by faith *(Habakkuk 2:4; Hebrews 10:38)*.

How do we know that the Blood has been applied to your heart? "But if we walk in the light as He is in the light, we have fellowship with one another, and the blood of Jesus Christ His Son cleanses us from all sin." *1 John 1:7*. If you are willing to walk in the light and allow the sanctifying work of the Holy Spirit to expose all the darkness in you, then you know that the Blood has been applied to your heart. (*Psalm 139:23-24, 2 Timothy 3:16-17)*.

I have used the phrase "I plead the Blood" because others were saying it, but now I know this is not a scriptural term. Maybe it's based on *Revelation 12:11*, but now I realize there is no need for me to plead the Blood. To "plead" is to beg, implore, etc.; it seems to put us in a defensive mode. "Pleading the Blood" is not necessary to defeat Satan. Revelation: Satan has already been defeated. Jesus came to destroy the works of the devil *(1 John 3:8)*. Death is the last enemy to be done away with *(1 Corinthians 15:26)*. Satan has no power over those who are born-again. So instead of "pleading the Blood", we should just do what *James 4:7* teaches, "Submit to God, Resist the devil and he will flee from you." Because we belong to Christ, we are already under His protection. "We" just need to trust Him day by day. So, I will say, "I proclaim the victory I have because of the Blood of Jesus Christ." *(1 Corinthians 15:57; Romans 8:37)*. I trust in the Power of God, not in the weakness of my flesh.

When we say, we overcome by the Blood of the Lamb and the word of our testimony, this is what our testimony to Satan is:

- Because the Blood of Jesus, I am redeemed out of the hand of the devil. (Ephesians 1:7; 1 Peter 1:18-19; Revelation 5:9; Psalm 107:2)

- Because the Blood of Jesus, all my sins are forgiven. (Colossians 2:13)

- Because the Blood of Jesus, I am continually being cleansed from all sin. (1 John 1:7)

- Because the Blood of Jesus, I am justified, made right

with God. (Romans 5:9)

- Because the Blood of Jesus, I am sanctified, made holy, set apart to God. (Hebrews 13:12)

- Because the Blood of Jesus, my body is a temple of the Holy Spirit. (1 Corinthians 6:19-20)

- Because the Blood of Jesus, Satan has no place in me, no power over me. (Hebrews 2:14)

- Because of the Blood of Jesus, my debt is Paid in Full. (Hebrew 9:28).

King David wrote in *Psalm 103:1-4*: Bless the LORD, O my soul: and all that is within me, bless his holy name. Bless the LORD, O my soul, and forget not all his benefits: Who forgiveth all things iniquities; Who healeth all thy diseases; Who redeemeth thy life from destruction; Who crowneth thee with lovingkindness and tender mercies; ~KJV

New Life in Christ by Faith

Chapter Five

Remember the story of the Philippian jailer in the Book of *Philippians 16:25-31?* In verses 29 and 30, he came trembling and fell down before Paul and Silas asking what he must do to be saved. They told him to believe on the Lord Jesus Christ, and he and his family would be saved. The jailer and his entire family were saved that night because they believed. The basic concept behind being saved or salvation is deliverance from the penalty of sin (death and separation from God) and the power of sin. We receive new life by faith, because we believe the finished work of Jesus.

The new life is a free gift from God. No one can ever earn this gift. The new life is based on the death of Christ on Calvary's Cross *(Romans 6:23)*. He was separated from the Father in order that we can be reconciled back to the Father. The new life can only be received by faith. "For it is by grace you have been saved, through faith and this not from yourselves, it is a gift from God." *(Ephesians 2:8)*. The new life received by faith is believing that Jesus died for our sins and that He took our place on the cross; however, this is not automatic.

In our old condition, we were dead to God. We were His enemy. In our ignorance, we walked/lived according to this world's system and the power of darkness. But being born again we have a new condition being alive to God. Therefore, we put off the old man and we put on the new man which is created in righteousness and the holiness of the truth and new in the spirits of our minds (*Ephesians 4:17-24*).

The new life in Christ can recognized through the reading and studying the Bible. The Bible is the road map to the proper instruction that is needed for the new life. It is the believers' mirror for the soul and spirit. God Himself gives inspiration for the writing of this book to the various authors. Second *Timothy 3:16* states that All scripture is given by inspiration of God. You could say it is the Manufacturer's User Guide. We can find answers for life's challenges, comfort in the time of sadness, peace, and guidance when we are confused and don't know what to do. We can find out what God loves, what He hates, what pleases Him, and what does not. If we need correction and discipline (rebuke for our sins), it is in the Bible. Simply put, the Bible is the authority of God for daily living, encouragement, and inspiration. Apostle Paul wrote in *2 Timothy 2:15*, "Study to shew thyself approved unto God, a workman that needeth not to be ashamed, rightly dividing the word of truth." God, our Creator and Father has provided the Bible so that we might know Him. He desires that all be saved and come to the knowledge of the truth *(1 Timothy 2:4; 2 Peter 3:9)*. The Bible contains spiritual riches that no other book can offer. It is profitable, for doctrine, for reproof, for correction, for instruction in righteousness (*2 Timothy 3:16*) so that we may live a holy life, well pleasing to God, that honors Him.

The more I read and study the Bible, the more I understand God's way of salvation. The Bible is one of the best aids in our journey of the new life. We can even gauge our growth and know if we are living a life pleasing and acceptable to God. We can conduct ourselves courageously for the Christ by imitating *(1 Corinthians 11:1)* Him and having the mind of Christ *(1 Corinthians 2:16)*.

Because this new birth leads to new life, we must pursue holiness. And pursuing holiness is growing in the grace and knowledge of Christ Jesus, our Lord. What comes to mind when you hear the word holy (holiness)? Some people have the wrong concept about being holy. The definition of holy is to cut, to sever, or to separate. God is separate and alone from everything else. He is separate from creation, because He is the Sovereign Creator. Holiness means for us to separate from the world's way of thinking and behaving; we pursue holiness by leaving the old sins behind and actively moving towards God *(John 17:16)*.

I have heard the statement that a person is "so heavenly minded that they are no earthly good". But Colossians teaches us we are to seek and set our affections on things in heaven where Christ is seated at the right hand of God (3:1-2). Holiness, should not be used in a negative light. God commands His people to be holy because He is holy *(1 Peter 1:15-16; Leviticus 20:16; 11:44)*. Biblical principles are to be taught, preached, and lived by those who are following Christ. There should not be any stumbling blocks placed in people's growth. The Bible teaches that "whosoever shall be a stumbling block to one of these little ones that believe in me *(Mark 9:42)*.

God did not send Jesus to rearrange us, but to transform and liberate us. He does not rearrange our deadness, but He changes our deadness to life as a new creature with a new nature. Everything changes: thoughts, values, agendas, etc. From the moment we are born again, we became partakers of the divine nature and escaped the world's corruption caused by human desires *(2 Peter 1:4)* – because we are changed from the inside out; our hearts have been circumcised. God has not called us to uncleanness but to holiness *(1 Thessalonians 4:7)*. The child of God is free to live a life that is consistent with their faith.

As faith believers, we have to realize that true repentance shows evidence of change. This is more than just merely expressing deep regret and remorse. It is changing our minds and changing our ways. This change before a holy God is going to be painful. It is not the easiest thing to have our sins exposed. Our spiritual life should be conforming to the image of Jesus Christ *(Romans 6-8)*. We can learn how to be delivered from sin. We can learn how to live a balanced life under grace. We can learn how to live the victorious Kingdom life through the power of the Holy Spirit, the Blood of Jesus, the Grace of God, and the Word of God.

I believe one of the greatest tragedies in life is for someone to go to church all of his or her life and are not saved. So, when she or he stands before God, he or she will hear Him say, "Depart from Me, I never knew you" *(Matthew 7:21-23)*. Yet, this is exactly what "a form of godliness" does to people. It is a great deception from the enemy that lets people lower their standards of life. It lets people justify their character traits, make excuses for their selfish lifestyles, live in sin, and persecute the believers of the truth, and condemn others who walk in righteousness.

Sadly, they really believe they have a right to speak on God's behalf. They are blinded to the truth of God and this leads them be "lovers of themselves, lovers of money, boasters, proud, blasphemers, disobedient to parents, unthankful, unholy, unloving, unforgiving, slanderers, without self-control, brutal, despisers of good, traitors, headstrong, haughty, lovers of pleasures rather than lovers of God." (*2 Timothy 3:2-4*). When we live a godly life, we have the power and authority in our life to do that which is right in the sight of the Lord (*Exodus 15:16; Deuteronomy 28:1-14*). We have been given the Holy Spirit to empower us. I don't believe Jesus came into the world to pay the supreme sacrifice and price of redemption for mankind for His power not to be demonstrated.

New life in Christ by faith means we have to cultivate our Christian Character. In *2 Peter 1*, we are taught how to do this. First, God has already given us everything that pertain to life and godliness (*vs. 3*). We have been given the promises of God that we might be partakers of His divine nature (*vs. 4*). We are to grow in Christ by adding to our faith virtue; to virtue knowledge; to knowledge self-control; to self-control patience; to patience godliness; to godliness brotherly kindness; brotherly kindness love (*vv. 5-7*). When these traits are cultivated in our character, we are fruitful in the knowledge of Jesus Christ, our Lord. To not cultivate our Christian character is to be blind and forget we were purged of our old sins (*vs. 9*). So, Peter urges us as believers to give diligence to make our calling [to be saints] and our relationship with God sure, that way we shall never fall or stumble (*vs. 10*).

It is said that we sin every day, but I want to know why? The Bible teaches me that sin separates us from God. No matter the degree of sin, it separates us from God, and that separation is death. God told Adam that the day he disobeys Him (eat from the tree of good and evil), he would die. In other words, Adam could no longer be in the presence of a holy God (*Genesis 3:3*). Sin's penalty, death, is remedied by life, union with God, which is achieved by believing in Jesus (*Romans 5:21*) Belief in Jesus breaks the penalty of sin. It may be probable to sin as a believer, but it is not necessary to do so (*1 John 2:1*). In saying this, sin should never be condoned nor excused by saying we are "only human." There are only two things we should do about sin: Confess it and forsake it (*Psalm 32:5*). [See *Psalm 51 and 1 John 1:9*]. To confess means to acknowledge or say the same thing as God says. In the believer's case, it means to say the same thing as God says about our sin: "It is sin." God is faithful. He is just to forgive of sins and cleanse from all unrighteousness *(1 John 1:9)*. The only unforgiven sin is the unconfessed sin. Then we have to forsake that sin and yield and submit completely to God by presenting our bodies as a living sacrifice which is our reasonable service (*Romans 12:1*).

I know there are times when our sinful, old nature will try to cause us to stumble in thought and deed. However, God has given us solutions to that. We can discipline our bodies as Apostle Paul did in *1 Corinthians 9:27*.

Freedom in Christ means freedom to generate the fruits

of righteousness through a life led by the Spirit. We are saved by the Gospel of Faith and Gospel of Grace. We start in faith, and our growth must continue in faith by grace (*Galatians 3:15*).

We are set free from the bondage of sin because of the power of the indwelling Spirit, but this liberty does not give us the excuse to yield to the flesh. Because there will be conflict between the Spirit and flesh, we must walk in the Spirit (*Galatians 5:16*), for that will empower us not to fulfill the lust of the flesh. *James 1:15* states, "Then when lust hath conceived, it bringeth forth sin and sin, when it is finished, bringeth forth death." The works of the flesh are manifest as adultery, fornication, uncleanness, and lasciviousness. It's having a complete disregard for the integrity and honor of others. (See *Ephesians 5:3*). The manifestation of the fruit of the Spirit is "But the first of the Spirit is love, joy, peace, longsuffering, gentleness, goodness, faith, meekness, temperance." (*1 Timothy 1:9*). If we therefore, have been baptized in Christ, we are to put on Christ (*Galatians 3:27*). I have to believe the Word of God Works; it does what it says it will do.

As children of God, we are to help one another when anyone is overtaken in a fault. *Galatians 6* states, "Brethren if a man be overtaken in a fault, ye which are spiritual, restore such an one in the Spirit of meekness. Considering thyself, lest thou also be tempted. Bear ye one another's burdens, and so fulfill the law of Christ (*VV.1-2*). Therefore, it is my aim that we all grow in our Christian faith so that our lives glorify God. We are part of the same body of Christ. "From whom the whole body fitly joined together and compacted by that which every joint supplieth, according to the effectual working in the measure of every part, maketh increase of the body unto the building up of itself in love." *(Ephesians 4:16)*.

Since we have received the Spirit of adoption, we are to reckon ourselves dead to sin but alive unto God through Jesus Christ our Lord *(Romans 6:11)*. We practice this when we yield our bodies as instruments of righteousness *(Romans 6:13)*. Once Jesus freed us from sin, we became obedient unto righteousness *(Romans 6:16)*. Those who walk in disobedience have not submitted themselves to the righteousness of God *(Romans 10:3)*. We sing that hymn "At the cross, at the cross". The Cross of Christ should bring us a message of change. The lives of believers should be different than the surrounding world. We should be a peculiar people, chosen by God *(1 Peter 2:9)*.

The Apostle Paul teaches us in Ephesians to put off the old man [Adam]. In other words, stop living as you once lived, in your own thinking and your own way *(4:17)* because you have now received Christ through the gospel. Put off the former life of the old man (nature) *(4:19-22)*. Be made new in your mind by putting on the new nature that God has created in righteousness and true holiness *(4:23-24)*. Therefore, demonstrating what is pleasing unto the Lord *(5:10)* by having "no fellowship with the unfruitful works of darkness" *(vs. 11)*, but rather, walk as children of the Light. "Awake thou that sleepest, and arise from the dead, and Christ shall give the Light *(vs. 14; Isaiah 26:19; 60:1)*.

Our provision for being children of the Light is being

filled with the Spirit. "But be filled with the Spirit." (Ephesians 5:18). In the original Greek, this verse is telling us to continually be filled with the Spirit. It is a lifelong process. When the Bible teaches about being filled with the Spirit, it means being controlled by the Spirit, not as a puppet, but a willing vessel. We must not confuse the indwelling of the Spirit with the filling of the Spirit. The filling is a repeated experience. Being filled is a command to be obeyed. The Spirit-filled person will exhibit the Christ-like character listed in *Galatians 5:22*. The Christian's life should reflect that Christ is first and foremost in their life. When we are rooted in Him *(Ephesians 3:17)*, alive in Him *(Romans 6:11)*, hidden in Him *(Colossians 3:3)*, and complete in Him *(Colossians 2:9)*.

I believe, as Believers, we can think too lowly and/or too earthly. I have heard before that a person can be so heavenly minded that he or she is no earthly good. This is false teaching. I believe that a person can be so earthly minded that she or he is no heavenly good. I base this on *Colossians 3:1-2*, "If ye then be risen with Christ, seek those things which are above, where Christ sitteth on the right hand of God. Set your affection on things above, not on things on the earth." Because Believers have risen with Christ, they are no longer citizens of this world *(John 17:16)*.

Colossians is one of my favorite Books of the Bible. In it Apostle Paul encourage believers to "continue in the faith grounded and settled" *(1:23)*, so that they will grow and bear fruit in the knowledge of Christ. We must not just be hearers of the word but doers also. The Bible is the Believers manual on how to live to produce fruit in their practical conduct

(Colossians 3 & 4). In other words, the Believer must consider himself dead to old sins and now consider himself alive to Christ in righteousness *(Colossians 3:5-11; 3:12-17)*. "Furthermore then we beseech you, brethren, and exhort you by the Lord Jesus, that as ye have received of us how ye ought to walk and to please God, so ye would abound more and more *(1 Thessalonians 4:1)*.

Because of the New Life in Christ by faith:

- We are accepted in the beloved. [*Ephesians 1:6*]

- We are blessed with all spiritual blessings. [*Ephesians 1:3*]

- We are chosen in Christ. [*Ephesians 1:4*]

- We are delivered from dark powers. [*Colossians 1:13*]

- We are elevated to heavenly places in Christ Jesus. [*Ephesians 2:6*]

- We are forgiven of all my sins. [*Ephesians 1:7*]

- We are God's workmanship. [*Ephesians 2:10*]

- We are healed by His Stripes. [*1 Peter 2:24*]

- We are Justified by faith. [*Romans 5:1*]

- We are kept by the power of God. [1 Peter 2:24]

- We are loved unconditionally. [*John 3:16*]

- We are more than a conqueror. [*Romans 8:37*]

- We are not condemned. [*Romans 8:1*]

- We are overcoming the world. [*1 John 5:5*]

- We are predestined to sonship. [*Ephesians 1:5*]

- We are made alive together with Christ. [*Ephesians 2:5*]

- We redeemed from the curse of the law. [*Galatians 3:13*]

- We are risen with Him [*Colossians 3:1-2*]

- We are sealed with the promised of the Holy Spirit. [*Ephesians 2:5*]

- We are unto His glory. [*Ephesians 1:14*]

- We are victorious through Jesus. [*1 Corinthians 15:57*]

- We are crucified with Christ. [*Galatians 2:20*]

- We are yoked together with believers. [*2 Corinthians 6:14*]

- We are Zealous of good works. [*Titus 2:14*]

New Identity in Christ

Chapter Six

First, we are made new in Christ. *2 Corinthians 5:17* states, "Therefore if any man [be] in Christ, [he is] a new creature: old things are passed away; behold, all things are become new." [KJV]. I believe this is still a subject some Christians really don't fully understand. Some think that they are saved and still remain the old creature, but that is not what Scripture teaches us. Our sins have been completely and eternally put away and removed from us. Through the gift of grace with have forgiveness of sin *(Colossians 2:13)* and are justified *(Romans 3:26, Galatians 2:16)*. The born-again believer is no longer under condemnation. They are deemed righteous in the eyes of God. When a person has been justified, it is as if they never sinned. Thus, the statement we are made new in Christ.

We are complete in Christ with grace to succeed. When we become children of the Most High God, we are given all we need in Christ to become spiritually mature believers *(Ephesians)*. It is up to us to choose to apply the principles of God in our lives with the help of the Spirit. When we comply, and conform to God's sanctifying process through the Holy Spirit, transformation will take place. There will be a change, inwardly as well as outwardly. We don't have to worry about changing ourselves, because it is God that does the changing. We just have to humbly submit and surrender to the Holy Spirit and study His Word.

There is a spiritual maturity that happens living in Christ. This maturity is by the grace of God alone, who is our source. Apostle Peter wrote that "His divine power has given us everything we need for life and godliness through our knowledge of Him who called us by His own glory and goodness *(2 Peter 1:30)*. So, our response is to grow in the grace and knowledge of our Lord and Jesus Christ.

When our identity is in Christ, it is one of newness *(2 Corinthians 5:17)*. We are no longer regarded as having the same old nature before we were born again. With the new nature, we began to take on recognizable characteristics of Christ. We should notice a change as well as others. We are different in our condition and our position. We are change from condemned sinners to saints as privileged sons. We now are heirs of God and joint heir with Christ *(Romans 8:17)*.

The definition of identity is the quality or condition of being the same as something (or someone) else. In the believer's case, our lives should indicate or demonstrate that we are the same as Christ or Christ like. When we use the term "Christians" it literally means "Followers of Christ". Our relationship with God changes because our identity in Christ. We are now reconciled to God *(Romans 5:10)*. Instead of the wrath of God, we have the love of God and are adopted as sons *(Romans 8:15-16)*. And we have the privilege of coming to God as "Pa Pa Father" *(Romans 8:15-16)*.

Having our new identity in Christ we are no longer slaves to sin (Romans 6:6). We no longer yield our body to be instruments of unrighteousness unto sin, but yield ourselves as instruments of righteousness unto God *(Romans 6:13)*.

Grace allows us to be set free from sin. And sin will NEVER outgrow grace (*Romans 5:20*). Grace wasn't given so that we continue to sin, but so we can be free not to sin (*Romans 6:14*). God does not or cannot pretend sin doesn't exist or look at us and make excuse for us. God has to have a plan in place to break sin's power over us and so we could be reconciled to Him. We lacked righteousness and God imputed the righteousness of Christ on those who believe and received His gift (*Romans 3:22*); *2 Corinthians 5:21*). Let's not frustrate the grace of God (*Galatians 2;21*).

Our identity in Christ calls us to be saints (*Romans 1:7*). We are called to belong to Jesus Christ (*Romans 1;6*). If we were indeed baptized into Christ, (*Romans 6:3*) our old man was crucified with Christ so that the body of sin might be destroyed that we should no longer sin (*Romans 6:6*).

I know there are those who say that no one is perfect or we are human. However, this is not a reason to keep habitually sinning. We sing about the blood of Jesus that never loses its power. Or the blood that gives me strength from day to day. Is this just a part of the formality of coming to church? Is it not believing that there is power in the blood of Christ? Whose report will we believe? No, I am not being judgmental, but I am trying to show that as long as this type of belief system goes on, then the blood won't be allowed to help. Apostle Paul said it is "a form of godliness, but denying its power" (*2 Timothy 3:5*). The blood of Jesus continually cleanses us from all sin. We are given the power to overcome the temptations (*1 Corinthians 10:13*).

The power of the gospel of grace is to those who believes

(*Romans 1:16*). When there is no evidence of the new nature, carnality is still involved in that person's life. I once read that "the emptiest and unhappiest occupation in the world is trying to act like a Christian when you are not a Christian." No one can serve two masters (*Matthews 6:24*).

God did not send His only begotten Son to suffer and die so that those who profess Christ can stay in their sin. God saves our soul and brings us out of darkness to bring us into His marvelous light (*1 Peter 2:9*). Therefore, we should not live as a child of the kingdom of darkness, but live as a child of the kingdom of light. Get into the Word of God and let His Word dwell in you. I believe there is truly power in the name of Jesus that He is able to make all grace abound (*2 Corinthians 9:8*) in our life. If you believe that name saves, then believe it can keep you from continually and habitually sinning. There is power for salvation and transformation.

If you don't have the Spirit of Christ, you don't belong to Him. Because if Christ is indeed in you, then you would be dead to sin (*Romans 8:9-10*). Spiritual life begins with spiritual birth and that birth (or rebirth) happens when we put our faith in Jesus Christ as Savior and Lord. The belief in Christ should be made known in the way we conduct our lives. We should practice righteousness and love for one another. There has to be an inward change with an outward show. The greatest proof to me of the new life is a changed life; a transformed and delivered life. After conversion, there should be a love of Jesus like never before. And this love causes you to love what He loves and hate what He hates. This love causes you to be obedient to what He says (*1 John 5:1-3*).

Your love for reading and studying the Bible should increase *(Psalm 119)*. Because the Word of God is profitable for doctrine, for reproof, for correction, for instructions in righteousness *(2 Timothy 3:16)*. Remember they that "hunger and thirst after righteousness shall be fed" *(Matthew 5:6)*. This love for Christ will make you love other believers. When you love other Christians, you know you have passed from death to life *(1 John 3:14)*. Then everyone will know that we are His disciples *(John 13:35)*. You will even love those who are your enemies *(Matthew 5:43-45)*. You will care about people's soul and where they will spend eternity and cry out like Apostle Paul in *Romans 10:1*. You will only serve one master with a pure life, loving the things of God not the things of the world *(1 John 2:15-17)*.

The Church of God in Christ Jesus

Chapter Seven

We can't really talk about the new life without including the Church, the Body of Christ. So, I want to discuss the church better known as the Body of Christ. This is the church that scripture describes. So, I am not talking about denominations or non-denominations because these are labels that have been systematically set by those who disagree with someone else's way of thinking or traditions or doctrines. The church was a mystery in the Old Testament. It was hidden and not revealed. It was prophesied in *Matthew 16:18*).

I found out that the rise of denominations within Christian faith goes back to the Protestant Reformation, the movement to "reform: The Roman Catholic Church during the 16th century. Out of that "reform" four major divisions or traditions of Protestantism emerged: Lutheran, Reformed, Anabaptist and Anglican. Consequently, out of these four divisions or denominations others grew over the centuries. Denominations come out of differences of opinion according to their conscience and their understanding of the Word of God. There is the difference in worship style, in the order of service, if women should be allowed to preach and teach, the way one dresses, if you should be baptized in the name of the Father, the Son, the Holy Ghost or in the name of Jesus, and the list goes on. I believe it is safe to say that denominations are the results of or caused by conflicts and confrontations which leads to division and separation. Jesus never intended for this to happen. But He calls for unity in the Body of Christ. This was and still is His prayer for all believers to be one (*John 17:21-22*).

Diversity is a good thing but disunity is not. There is an example of this in the Epistle to the church at Corinth which was struggling with issues of division and separation. Apostle Paul addresses this in *1 Corinthians 1:12-13*. Quarrels had broken out among the church. Some were saying they follow Paul or they Apollos, or they follow Cephas or they follow Christ. So, Paul asked these questions for thought: "Is Christ divided into groups? Was Paul crucified for you? Or were you baptized in the name of Paul?" Apostle Paul understood the importance of promoting a spirit of unity in the face of disorder and disunity. In Christ, there is only ONE Church and ONE body of believers. And I personally believe that anything less or different weakens and destroys the unity and power of the church.

The word church is used in five ways: a building designated as a place of worship and fellowship, the building; all who profess faith in Christ; a denomination; a single organized Christian group and the Body of Christ (the universal church). But I want to deal with the true Body of Christ, the saints of God. The group of people who are called out from among the rest of the people. This is actually those who have put their faith in Jesus for their salvation because they could not save themselves and are disciples of Him. Jesus has now become Savior and Lord of their life. The Body of Christ like our bodies have parts that have specifically assigned parts, but not separate from each other but as a unit. *1 Corinthians 12:12-14* states it like this:" The body is a unit, though it is made up of many parts, and though all its parts are many parts, they form one body. So, it is with Christ. For we were all baptized by One Spirit into one body. Whether Jews or Greeks, slave or free-and we were all given the One Spirit to drink. Now the body is not made up of one part but of many." So, no matter what part you are called into, everyone has an equal part of the body of the Christ. Apostle Paul wrote this to the Ephesians: And God placed all things under His feet and appointed him to be head over everything for the church, which is his body, the fullness of him who fills everything in every way." *1:22-23*) Do you see that the church is the fullness of Christ? That is such an awesome truth.

In the book of *Acts 7:38*, the church was used for the nation of Israel, which were a group of people who were called out from the rest of the people of the world as His chosen people; His treasured possession (*Deuteronomy 7:6*) in order to have a special national relationship with God. The Bible shows the local church is a visible, temporary manifestation of the universal church. The universal church is made up of all believers from the disciples once Jesus was resurrected until the time He comes back to take the church out of the world. At the day of Pentecost, the local church and the universal church were identical. The three thousand souls added to the group that continued in the apostle's doctrine, fellowship, and breaking of bread were together *(Acts 2:41-47)*. I believe this is the example for the church today. They didn't do anything until they were empowered by the Holy Spirit. Jesus had instructed them to wait in Jerusalem for the promise of the Father, which was the Holy Spirit *(Acts 1:4)*. On the appointed day and time, the Holy Spirit came in and fill the house where they sat. The Holy Spirit came and sat or rested on them and they were all filled. The Holy Spirit transformed this group of 120 from those who were fearful into bold witnesses of Jesus Christ. The disciples were transformed and filled with courage and boldness to proclaim the message of the resurrected savior, Jesus Christ. This small group became a thriving, worldwide church that the Lord added to daily of those who should be saved *(Acts 2:47)* thus fulfilling the Great Commission *(Matthew 28:18-20)* with the help of the Holy Spirit *(Acts 1:8)*. The Holy Spirit is for the church of today as well.

Church attendance was very important from the 120 gathering in the upper room to those meeting from house to house *(Acts 2:46)*. So, it is still very important today to assemble together as believers. *Hebrews 10:25* shows we have an obligation to one another. WE are to provoke one another to good works and to exhort one another to live consistent lives worthy of God. Some people believe they don't need to attend church or they can listen to the radio or watch church service on the television. But I believe this type of thinking is a deception of the enemy and lack of knowledge of the Word of God. (now I am not talking about those who cannot attend church for some medical reason.) In the church, I attend we rehearse the Church Covenant together. The last paragraph states: "When we remove from this place, we engage as soon as possible to unite with some other church where we can carry out the spirit of this covenant and the principles of God's Word." We are to endeavor to keep the unity of the Spirit in the bond of peace (*Ephesians 4:3-6*). The writer of *Psalms 133* states how good and pleasant it is when believers dwell together in unity. There is a blessing in being united unto One Lord, One faith, and One baptism (*Ephesians 4:5-6*).

There is a difference between church members and disciples of Christ or church goers and Christ followers. A church member can be anyone who has some religion, a respect for Jesus, attends church, leads a "good" life or tithe every Sunday. They may even know a few scriptures. They may even work in the church. A disciple is someone who has been converted and regenerated with the primary aim in life to follow Jesus. In fact, Jesus states that you can't be His disciples unless you follow Him daily (*Matthew 16:24-27; Mark 8: 34-37; Luke 9:22-26*).

There is often a big misunderstanding about the two. So, everyone who attends church are classified as Christians. But everyone who calls themselves Christians aren't followers of Christ. Remember the Bible teaches about the wheat and tare growing up together in the parable in *Matthew 13:24-30*. It is important for those who confess to belong to Christ be a witness of Christ. And the way we can be that witness is to love one another as Jesus love us. Jesus told His disciples recorded in *John 13: 34-35* "A new commandment I give unto you, that ye love one another, as I have loved you that ye also love one another. By this shall all men know that ye are my disciples, if you have love one to another. In other words, the love we show towards each other sets us apart and God is glorified.

Then *1 Corinthians 12:27-28* goes on to teach: "Now you are the body of Christ, and each of you is a part of it. And in the church God has appointed first of all apostles, second prophets, third teachers, then workers of miracles, also those having gifts of healing, those able to help others, those with gifts of administration, and those speaking in different kinds of tongues. Does this look like today's church? Because there is not an operation of the parts of the body, the church is suffering and weak. Although God is the one who appoints these roles, they aren't allowed to be in full operation in the church. Could it be that the leaders are ignorant to this or just rebellious? I will say this; it is not God's fault because He has given the Body of Christ everything that is needed for Kingdom purpose. God has given every member of the body a gift(s) to be used for service to build it up and strengthen it so that it can carry out its purpose. When the diversity of gifts supports each other, it makes the body strong. Why is the church in general still weak? I believe this is part of the reason found in this verse from *1 Corinthians 14:26*, "When you come together, everyone has a hymn, or a word of instruction, a revelation, a tongue or an interpretation. All of these must be done for the strengthening of the church." As born-again believers in Christ, the question should be asked, "As a member of this holy entity, the body, how can I enhance or strengthen the church?"

So many times, it seems that we forget the real purpose of being a part of Christ's Body. I make this statement because we put each other down. We gossip about each other. We are jealous of each other. We have malice towards one another. We put our standards on each other. We judge and misjudge each other by being judgmental. We assume the worst of each other. We sow discord between each other. We are suspicious of each other. Our hearts are cold towards each other. We hinder the growth of the knowledge of the Lord in each other. All causing the Body of Christ to be disjointed, disconnected, dysfunctional, deceived and weak.

This is not the intended plan of God for His church, local (*Matthew 18:17; Acts 15:4*) or universal (*Matthew 16:18; Acts 20:28; Ephesians 2:21-22*). We are supposed to be an assembly of people called together as God's people in Christ. We are called together as citizens of the Kingdom of God (*Ephesians 2:19*) for the purpose of worshiping the One and Only True God. When God's people come together in one voice to praise Him and give Him thanks, we make a place for Him to visit or show up and when the glory comes no one can work (*2 Chronicles 5:12-14*).

As the church of God in Christ, we are called out of the world and into the Kingdom of God. Because we are the temple of the Holy Spirit (*Ephesians 2:11-22*). We, as the church, is a spiritual fellowship with God and one another (*2 Corinthians 13:14; Philippians 2:1; 1 John 1:3*). This spiritual fellowship is based on the indwelling of the Holy Spirit (*Luke 11:13; John 7:37—39; 20:22*); the unity of the Holy Spirit (Ephesians 4:4); and the baptism of the Holy Spirit (*Acts 1:5; 2:4; 8:14-17; 10:44; 19:1-7*). The Holy Spirit enables the church to be a spiritual ministry by use of gifts (*Romans 12:6; 1 Corinthians 1:7; 12:4-11; 28-31' Ephesians 4:11*). And also by the cultivation of the fruit of the Spirit in the church. "But the fruit of the Spirit is love, joy, peace, forbearance, kindness, goodness, faithfulness, gentleness and self-control." (*Galatians 5:22-23*). These attributes or characteristics are produced in God's children as they allow the Holy Spirit to direct and influence their lives. This cultivation works in destroying sin's power and enabling the children of God to walk in fellowship with Him when we seek and submit to the Holy Spirit (*Romans 8:5*). Then truly we will be walking in love towards one another and the world will see it and know that we are disciples of Christ (*John 13:35*).

The Marks of the Sheep

Chapter Eight

"My sheep hear my voice, and I know them, and they follow me."
John 10:27

The Gospel of John states the marks of a sheep in the 10th Chapter. In verse one, Jesus points out that the only way to be a sheep is if one enters by the door. The sheep hears the voice of the Shepherd. In verse three, the gatekeeper opens the gate. Just like Jesus is the Shepherd, the Holy Spirit is the Gatekeeper. Any other way, that person is classified as a thief and a robber (*John 10:1*), those who enter illegally. Remember when Jesus told the parable of the wedding feast in *Matthew 22:1-14*. There was a gentleman that got in and was approached about his attire. Now I know this is not a parable about clothes, but I wanted to point out that no one enters in another way and not be noticed. When he was asked about his clothes, he didn't have an answer. So, he was thrown outside. Those who enter by the door has been clothed with the righteousness of Christ. God has provided a covering for our sin. No one can legally enter by the door by their own self-righteousness or by works. *Ephesians 2:8* confirms this: "For by grace you have been saved through faith; and that not of yourselves. It is the gift of God; not as a result of works, so that no one may boast."

John 8:12 teaches us that Jesus is the light of the world and if we follow Him we will not walk in darkness. So, there can be victory for us when we follow Jesus. He is our righteous

Advocate before the Father *(1 John 1:5-2:22)* and His blood continually cleanses us from all sin. No one is without sin before receiving salvation and forgiveness and justification, but thanks be to God we have been justified through the blood of Christ. As Jesus told the woman caught in adultery, "go and sin no more" *(John 8:11)*. I do believe the Lord expects us not sin no more through the help He has given us by the Holy Spirit.

Although the Lord is not slack concerning His promise, He is longsuffering and that longsuffering is salvation for He doesn't want anyone to perish but come to repentance (turn away from darkness and turn to the light). However, the day of the Lord will be like a thief that comes in the night. That is why Jesus exhorts the disciples. Therefore, we must grow in grace and not fall from our steadfastness *(2 Peter 3:9-18)*. Jesus told His disciples to watch and pray that they enter into temptation: the spirit is indeed wiling, but the flesh is weak *(Matthew 28:41)*. Only those who are in the light will not be caught off guard when He returns.

Though temptations come, if we abide in Christ we can have confidence and assurance before Him. Our confidence is that our sins are forgiven and we can enjoy fellowship with God through Jesus Christ. Because He is able to keep us from falling and present us faultless before God *(Jude 24)*. Being transformed into the likeness of Christ makes us incompatible with sin because sin is contrary to the person and work of Christ *(1 John 3:4-6)*. Our behavior of fellowship with God should reflect that we are abiding in Christ. That is insofar as we do so abide, we do not sin. So, saints of God, we can be certain that sin is a threat to fellowship and it should be regarded as foreign to our position in Christ (*1st John 5:18; Romans 6*). Because the Lord himself knows how to deliver the godly out any and all temptations (*2 Peter 2:9*). He is faithful to provide a way of escape out so we can endure it (*1 Corinthians 13:10*). Now that is reassuring to know. There has to be practice with professing. Because profession without practice is useless.

God has equipped you and I for a holy walk or holy way of living, but the choice is ours to make. After we have received the gift of salvation by believing and putting our faith in Jesus Christ and Him alone, we are to present ourselves to God as living sacrifices, totally committed; totally surrendered.

God's Amazing Grace

Chapter Nine

Growing in the new life requires grace. Grace means pure unrecompensed kindness and favor. We have to understand that growth comes by grace and it is God alone that supplies it. God is the source. The second epistle of Apostle *Peter 1:3-9* reminds us that God is the source. "His divine power has given us everything we need for life and godliness through our knowledge of him who called us by his own glory and goodness. When we became a child of God, we were given all we need "in Christ" to become spiritually maturing believer. We just have to submit to God's maturing process. He will conform us to the image of Jesus Christ as we humbly surrender to the Holy Spirit and study His Word. *Hebrews 13:20-21* says, "May the God of peace, who through the blood of the eternal covenant brought back from the dead our Lord Jesus, that great Shepherd of the sheep, equip you with everything good for doing his will, and may he work in us what is pleasing to him, through Jesus Christ, to whom be glory for ever and ever. Amen."

We are saved through grace by faith and we are His masterpiece that have been created in Christ Jesus. We were created unto good works. (*Ephesians 2:10*). Being born again we have been passed through Potter's creative hand a second time to become new creatures. Therefore, we can only have grace to succeed being created in Christ Jesus. God heaps grace upon grace, super abounding, and without measure. Because the believer who is perfectly saved from the guilt and penalty of sin needs to also be saved from the reigning power of sin. Through grace and the power of God the believer is always kept.

Christian growth can only happen with spiritual Christians. The immature believers are carnal in nature and is said to be an infant. Therefore, the believer that is saved by grace has to also stand in grace *(1 Peter 5:12)*. The Bible teaches that we should deny ungodliness and worldly lusts, and to live soberly, righteously, and godly. Through grace we have salvation from sin, death, and sufferings. For those who live according to the Spirit will mind the things of the Spirit *(Romans 8:5)*.

In the Christian community grace is simply defined as unmerited favor. And yes, that is true but in my study, it has been revealed that grace often represents that which is limitless. Grace is all-abundant *(Romans 5:15-20)*. Grace is manifold (1 Peter 4:10). Grace is all-sufficient *(2 Corinthians 12:9)*. The Grace that came by Jesus Christ *(John 1:17)* represents realties which are infinite and eternal. The measureless Grace is the unlimited eternal love of God. Scripture gives us the witness that God saves sinners by grace *(Ephesians 2:8-9)*. That saving grace goes beyond that. It is a keeping and empowering Grace. This Grace was given to us in Christ before the ages began *(2 Timothy 1:9)*.

We are God's workmanship created in Christ Jesus *(Ephesians 2:10)*. Notice that we are created in Christ Jesus. The new life in Christ, only. There is no other way but through Him that the saved entered into the new life. He is the Way, the Truth, and the Life (*John 14:6*). Jesus said that no one can come to the Father but by Him and no one comes unless the Father draws them. Any other way, that person enters as a thief and a robber.

Grace is something many talk about but may not fully understand it. We all know we don't deserve it nor can we earn it. Grace is what can change the reality of our day and even moment by moment. Grace is so amazing in that it shows how much God loves us. No matter how much a believer thinks that there are things they can do without God, it still doesn't mean that Grace is not at work. Believers are under grace (*Romans 6:14*). We all have received grace after grace because of His abundance (*John 1:16*). By faith we have access into grace where we now stand (*Romans 5:2*). Grace is limitless because God makes all grace abound unto us (*2 Corinthians 9:8*). No matter what comes our way, we can be strong in the grace that is in Christ Jesus (*2 Timothy 2:1*). We are to grow in grace and the knowledge of Christ (*2 Peter 3:28*). We are to even speak with wisdom so it will give grace to those who are listening (*Ephesians 4:29*).

The Bible teaches us two truths under grace: we are in Christ and Christ is in us. In other words, every child of God is vitally united to Christ. As born-again believers, we are placed in Christ by the indwelling of the Holy Spirit. "For by one Spirit are we all baptized into one body, whether we be Jews or Gentiles, whether we be bond or free; and have been all made to drink into the one Spirit (*1 Corinthians 12:13*). It is only the born-again believer not the unsaved that is in Christ. The very Spirit has baptized us into the body of Christ. Therefore, in the spiritual realm, Christ is the sphere of our position. We are seated in heavenly places in Christ Jesus (*Ephesians 2:6*). Christ encompasses, surrounds, encloses, and indwells us. We are in Christ and Christ is in us.

Our new life in Christ gives us our new positions:

- We are elect and called of God (*1 Thessalonians 1:4; 5:24*)
- We are redeemed by God through the blood of His Son (*Colossians 1; 14*)
- We are reconciled to God by the death of His Son (*2 Corinthians 5:19*)
- We are sheltered eternally under the propitiation made in the blood of Christ (*1 John 2:2*)
- We are forgiven all trespasses, past, present, and future (*Colossians 2:13*)
- We are no more condemned forever *(Romans 8:1)*
- We are justified freely by His grace (*Romans 3:24*)
- We are sanctified or set apart unto God in Christ (*1 Corinthians 1:30*)
- We are perfected forever (*Hebrews 10:14*)
- We are made meet to be a partaker of the inheritance of the saints in light (*Colossians 1:12*)
- We are made accepted in the Beloved (*Ephesians 1:6*)
- We are made the righteousness of God in Christ *(2 Corinthians 5:21)*
- We are made nigh to God in Christ (*Ephesians 2:13*)
- We are a child and son of God in Christ (*John 1:12; 1 John*

3:3)
- We are delivered from the power of darkness *(Colossians 2:13)*
- "But the God of all grace, who hath called us unto his eternal glory by Christ Jesus, after that ye have suffered a while, make you perfect (complete), stablish, strengthen, settle you" *(1 Peter 5:10)*

Our new standing in Christ include all the positions under grace which are "the riches of grace in Christ Jesus" *(Ephesians 2:7)*. May the eyes of our understanding be enlightened that we may know what is the hope of our calling and the riches of the glory of His inheritance in the saints *(Ephesians 1:18)*.

Our Christian character is not a product of the flesh. It is fruit of the Spirit *(Galatians 5:22-23)*. Apostle Paul wrote: "This I say then walk in the Spirit and ye shall not fulfill the lust of the flesh *(Galatians 5:16)*. As Believers, our responsibility is not the walk but the yielding to the Spirit who promotes the walk. As long as the walk is continued by the and in the power of the Spirit, the spiritual life will be successful. Because being Spirit-filled we glorify God in every moment of life. We must be watchful, steadfast, and unmovable while maintaining the attitude of co-operation with, yielding to and dependent on Holy Spirit by grace.

The new life in Christ by grace replaces the law with grace *(Romans 6:14)*. It replaces condemnation with salvation *(Romans 8:1)*. It replaces death with life *(Ephesians 2:1; Romans 5:10; John 5:2)*. It replaces destruction in Adam with regeneration in Christ (*Romans 5:12; 1 Corinthians 15:21*). It replaces bondage with liberty in Christ (*Galatians 5:1*). It replaces defeat with victory in Christ (*1 Corinthians 15:57*). It replaces hell with heaven (*Philippians 3:20; Hebrews 13:14-21*).

I believe the phrase "in Christ" has the greatest meaning to the born-again believer than any words pertaining to our faith. The believer's position has to be "in Christ". Believers are blessed with all spiritual blessings in Christ. With such a glorious relationship in Christ, it is the believer's responsibility to walk worthy of the calling they were called.

Unchangeable grace has brought believers into the new creation in Christ. As new creatures with a new nature, to be in Christ is to be in the sphere of His Eternal Person, Power and Glory. In this new position, Christ supplies in Himself all that one will ever need in time and eternity. Christ, alone, gives access into the grace of God (*John 1:17; Romans 5:2*) and there has to be a difference between an unsaved person's life and a saved person's life. Through Christ we have been imputed righteousness. Therefore, there should be the application of that righteousness. *Romans 8:4* states, that the "righteousness of the law" might be fulfilled in us, who walk not after the flesh, but after the Spirit. Once we believe in Jesus, I believe that our behavior must be built on that belief. Our life has to have an inward change with an outward witness of that change. I am not saying a changed life is a condition for salvation instead it should be the natural (supernatural) outcome of saving faith fulfilled in by the Spirit.

The working of grace helps us by the Holy Spirit to succeed in this Christian life. We have the divine enablement under grace. Grace, the all-powerful, abiding, indwelling and sufficient Holy Spirit of God has been given to every born-again believer. It is totally depending on the enabling power of the indwelling Spirit (*Acts 1:8*).

God's Grace is so amazing! This gift of Grace amazes as it offends. It is the grace that pays the same wages to the one who works all day or just a few hours of that day (*Matthew 20:10-16*). Grace runs towards the prodigal son/daughter clothed in sin and wraps him/her up and then throws a party without hesitation (*Luke 15:11-31*). It was Grace that Christ accepted the thief on the cross dying plea, "Please remember me when you have come into Your Kingdom" (*Luke 23:42)*. Today you will be with me in Paradise." The Grace that took pleasure in sending His Only Son to die for our sake *(John 3:16; Isaiah)*. Grace that is enough for our weakness. This Grace doesn't discriminate and doesn't play favoritism. It is a "whosoever" Grace. That means you and me. It works without or need our help. Grace is not cheap but it is free. Grace is enough because Grace is Jesus.

"So, I will celebrate my weakness, for when I'm weak, I sense more deeply the might power of Christ living in me (*2 Corinthians 12:9-10 TPT*). Why do we try to work that which grace is enough for? Why do we try to work for this generously pure grace? For grace is not grace if it does not work alone. Why do I hear so many say, I'm not worthy" when Jesus gave His life? He died and was buried; and when his resurrection shows us that it was not a matter of us being worthy but whether or not we will receive what he freely gives. "For when we were yet sinners, Christ died for the ungodly" (*Romans 5:8*). Grace is a gift that is feely given to all who would receive. Once we receive the pure Grace that is given, we have to accept it vulnerably and humbly into our hearts and our lives. Grace is enough and grace helps us succeed. In others words, the grace that shapes the Believer's life is the grace that makes the believer succeed. I read somewhere that grace is love that cares and stoops and rescues. Apostle Paul wrote in *Titus 2:11*, "the grace of God has appeared, bringing salvation for all people, training us to renounce ungodliness and worldly passions, and to live self-controlled, upright and godly lives."

We are urged to "grow in grace and knowledge of our Lord and Savior Jesus Christ *(2 Peter 2:18)*. Grace transforms our motives, our attitudes, our behavior, our desires, our character. God's grace through Jesus Christ, is at the care and center of the Bible.

1 Corinthians 1:10 teaches us that "By the grace of God I am what I am". We can say because of grace we have our Christian identity.

Romans 5:2 teaches us that "we access by faith into this grace which we stand". We can say grace gives our standing before God.

2 Corinthians 2:12 teaches, "we behaved in the …by the grace of God." We can say grace governs our behavior.

Romans 5:17 and *1 Peter 1:7* teaches those who receive "the abundance of grace and the free gift of righteousness reign in life through the One Man, Jesus Christ." ...by the "grace of life." We can the abundance of grace we live, move, and have our being in Christ.

2 Timothy 2:9 teaches God "called us to a holy calling ... because of His own purpose and grace." We can say we our living, holy, by grace because it is His purpose.

2 Timothy 2:1 teaches "be strengthened by the grace that is in Jesus Christ for: it is good for the heart to be strengthened by grace." We can by grace gives us strength in our hearts to have strength for living this called out life.

1 Peter 1:10 teaches "let your speech always be gracious." We can say grace governs our manner of speaking.

2 Corinthians 2:8-9 teaches "My grace is sufficient for you." "God is able to make all grace abound in every good work." We can that grace that grace is our sufficiency.

Hebrews 4:16 and *1 Peter 1:10* teaches we get "grace to help in time of need" and when "you have suffered a little while, the God of all grace will Himself, restore, confirm, strengthen, and establish you." We can say that grace is our response to difficulty and suffering.

1 Peter 1:13 teaches 'Set your hope fully on the grace that will be brought to you at the revelation of Jesus Christ." We can say that grace is our salvation.

Romans 5:21 teaches "grace (reigns) through righteousness leading to eternal life through Jesus Christ our Lord. We can say grace is our hope beyond death.

We, as believers, receive grace (*Acts 11:23*), encouraged to continue in grace (*Acts 13:43*) and are called to testify to the grace of God (*Acts 20:24*). Jesus says in *John 20:24*). Jesus says in *John 20:21*; "As the Father has sent me, even so I am sending you". God's "commission is for the entire world" (*Matthew 28:16-20*).

We are called by God's Grace because it pleased Him. (*Galatians 1;15; Isaiah 49:1,5; Jeremiah 1:5; Romans 1:1*). The grace of our Lord Jesus Christ be with you all. Amen. (*Revelation 22:21*)

Grace: the Power to Succeed

Chapter Ten

As born-again believers, we have been given the grace to succeed in Christ Jesus. *John 1:17* states that truth and grace came by Christ. It was given to us before time began. "This grace was given to us in Christ Jesus before the ages began." *2 Timothy 1:9*. Grace is so much more than undeserved favor. We may not fully grasp the full measure of God's grace, but it is sufficient for our needs *(2 Corinthians 12:9)*. We are the recipients of such an amazing gift. We cannot earn it. God's will for us is absolute good. Therefore, God's grace is available to everyone at all times and in all circumstances. Grace gives meaning and glory to our lives as members of the Body of Christ on earth.

Grace gives us the power and strength to have Christ formed in us. This is the goal of our new life in Christ. Apostle Paul's work in Galatia was to help Christ be formed in them *(Galatians 4:19)*. Through the renewing of our minds, we can be transformed into the likeness and image of Christ *(Romans 12:2)*. As Born-Again Believers, our desire to be like Christ. This is what salvation is all about. He gave His life for us and we give our lives to Him, daily. Ephesians teaches that we are to reach unity in the faith and knowledge of the Son of God and become mature, attaining to the whole measure of the fullness of Christ *(4:13)*.

Grace is given so that we can take off the old nature with its practices and put on the new nature. The new nature in

Christ has been created in true righteousness and holiness. This spiritual formation comes as we submit ourselves to God as instruments of righteousness. Christ is not formed in us by accident, we must turn to God in faith. It is up to us to make those choices that agree with the Word of God on how to live out this spiritual life in Christ. The transformation process is that a process. We give our lives to Him daily and He shapes us to become more like Him. *Jeremiah 18:4* states, "You are like the clay in the potter's hands, and I am the potter." This is our lifelong commitment that we have as Disciples of Christ. Our lives should be Christ-centered. We are Christ-like people and have a Christ-like job. We are the salt of the earth and the light of the world. We obey the commands of Jesus to love others, pray for others, help others that confirms we are following Him *(John 13:35)*.

Grace has divine motives for the salvation of sinners. *Ephesians 2:10* states, "For we are his workmanship, created in Christ Jesus unto good works, which God hath before ordained that we should walk in them." As His workmanship or masterpiece, our transformation is wholly done a work of God for man. It is God alone who save and God alone who can keep and sustain. We are "created in Christ Jesus" by the divine work by the hand of God a second time. We are created unto good works.

We have the limitless character of God's grace. The Bible gives us this information through the following scriptures:

• *John 1:16* teaches, "And of his fullness have all we received, and grace for [added to, or heaped upon] grace."

• *Romans 5:17* teaches, "Abundance [superabundance] of grace."

• *Romans 5:20* teachers, "But where sin abounded, grace did much more abound."

• *2 Corinthians 9:14* teaches, "And by prayer for you, which long after you for the exceeding [above measure] grace of God in you."

• *2 Corinthians 4:15* teaches, "The abundant [more than enough] grace."

• *Romans 5:2* teaches, "We have access by faith into this grace wherein we stand."

The true grace of God toward the believer is the one and only basis upon which he or she can hope to endure. There is no power found in the flesh or any other human resources. Our natural ability can no more maintain a right standing with God or before than it can attain such a standing. It is believing in Christ alone that we can secure this infinite grace of God.

Sovereign Grace gives us instruction for daily instruction and daily growth in our Christian faith in God (*Titus 2:11*). And our lives are to be governed only by the teachings of grace (*Galatians 6:16; Philippians 3:16*). There is no need to add to these instructions because the teachings of grace are perfect and sufficient in themselves. Theses teachings of grace is not only gracious in character, but they are extended to cover the entire range of life's issues of the Christian. Grace is given to have the capacity to change, tolerate, accommodate, and forgive. A Christian's conduct throughout life defines his or her growth (*Hebrews 6:1*). The first step towards growth is obedience to God. We choose to live by God's perspective instead of our own (*Galatians 5:16, 25*). It grows and matures as revelation increases. As new creations in Christ by faith, our response is to grow in grace. *Second Peter* teaches to grow in grace and the knowledge of Christ (*3:18*).

Through Grace we are:

• Elect and called of GOD (*1 Thessalonians 1: 4; 5: 24*).

• Redeemed by GOD through the blood of His Son (*Colossians 1: 14*).

• Reconciled to GOD by the death of His Son (*2 Corinthians 5:19*).

• Sheltered eternally under the propitiation made in the blood of CHRIST (*I John 2: 2*).

• Forgiven all trespasses, past, present, and future (*Colossians 2: 13*).

• Condemned no more forever (*Romans 8:1*).

- Justified freely by His grace (Romans 3: 24).
- Sanctified, or set apart unto GOD in CHRIST (*1 Corinthians 1:30*).
- Perfected forever (*Hebrews 10:14*).
- Made meet to be a partaker of the inheritance of the saints in light (*Colossians 1:12*).
- Made accepted in the Beloved (*Ephesians 1:6*).
- Made the righteousness of GOD in Him (*2 Corinthians 5:21*).
- Made nigh to GOD in CHRIST JESUS (*Ephesians 2:13*).
- A child and son of GOD (*John 1:12; I John 3: 3*).
- Free from the law and dead to the law (*Romans 7:4, 6*).
- Delivered from the power of darkness (*Colossians 1:13*).
- Translated into the kingdom of GOD's dear Son (*Colossians 1:13*).
- Founded on the Rock CHRIST JESUS (*1 Corinthians 3: 11*).
- GOD's gift to CHRIST (*John 17:11, 12, 20; 10:29*).
- Circumcised in CHRIST (*Colossians 2:11*).
- A holy priest, chosen, and peculiar (*I Peter 2:5, 9*).
- Object of divine love, grace, power, faithfulness, peace, consolation (*Ephesians 2: 4, 8: 1:9*)
- *Hebrews 13:5; Colossians 3:15; 2 Thessalonians 2:16*).

- Object of CHRIST's intercession *(Hebrews 7:25)*.
- His inheritance *(Ephesians 1:18)*.
- Seated in the heavenly in CHRIST *(Ephesians 2:6)*.
- A citizen of Heaven *(Philippians 3:20)*.
- Of the family and household of GOD *(Ephesians 2:19; 3:15)*.
- Light in the Lord *(Ephesians 5:8)*.
- In GOD, in CHRIST, and in the Spirit *(1 Thessalonians 1:1; John 14:20; Romans 8:9)*.
- Possessed with the first fruits of the Spirit. Born *(John 3:6)*,
- Baptized *(1 Corinthians 12:13)*, indwelt *(1 Corinthians 6:19)*, and sealed *(Ephesians 4:30)*.
- Glorified *(Romans 8:30)*.
- Complete in Him *(Colossians 2:10)*.
- Possessing every spiritual blessing *(Ephesians 1:3)*.

Heavenly Father, I surrender my heart to You. Help me to open my life and let you reign and rule over every aspect of it. Being made a new creation in Christ, give me a sensitive spirit to the Spirit of Grace that I may live glorifying you all the days of my life. In Jesus name, I pray. Amen.

Growing Spiritually in the New Life

Chapter Eleven

It is essential that we know and understand how to grow/mature spiritually. Growing in our new life is submitting to the lordship of Christ in reverence and service. *Galatians 5:16* teaches the Christian's life is walking in the spirit. This is a step by step process of the new life in Christ. In other words, living by the Spirit's power is a moment-by-moment yielding to His will and control. This process is called sanctification. And the evidence or manifestation of this yielding is the fruit of the Spirit (*Galatians 5:22*).

It is very naïve and irresponsible to think that we won't face problems in our new life. There will be problems both in our natural lives as well as our spiritual lives. As we go through these challenges, it should cause us to grow and be strengthened in the Lord, and this will bring glory to God. Because God is faithful and His grace is sufficient for every need (*2 Corinthians 12:9*). Our challenges give us the gateway to trust in Christ more and more. We also we know that Christ identifies with our sufferings (*Hebrews 4:15*).

Prayer is also essential in growing spiritually. Take time to develop passion and zeal for prayer life. Our Father wants to hear from you and answer your prayers. He wants to teach you how to pray. Prayer is also where you learn to recognize God's voice. Your prayer life is a very vital part communing and fellowshipping with God. It doesn't matter where you are, what time it is or what is going on, prayer allows you to talk with God without limitations. It can be done verbally or silently. *Hebrews 13:5* tells us that God will never leave or forsake us. Therefore, because He is always with us we can always engage in conversation with Him. Prayer is simply talking to God. *Psalm 62:8* tells us to "pour out your hearts to God." Prayer was the one thing that the disciples asked Jesus to teach them (*Luke 11:1*).

As believers, we must be mindful of the places, people, situations and times we may be vulnerable to temptation. However, even with problems of sin, temptation, suffering and doubt, we can have a remedy for them. We can choose to occupy our minds with the things of the Lord (*Colossians 3:1-4*). And the best way to do this is studying and understanding the word of God (*Romans 10:17*). The Word produces growth in faith. I believe the more we study the Word of God, the easier it is to desire the Word of God.

Jesus is the living Word and He lives His life in and through us as we walk in dependence upon Him (*John 1:11-12; 10:10; 15:4-5; Galatians 2:20*). Christ is Emanuel, God who dwells with us. In the beginning the Word was made flesh and dwelt among us. In Christ, God revealed Himself in human flesh. Therefore, to see Christ is to see God (*John 12:45; 14:9*); to know Christ is to know God (*John 8:19*); to receive Christ is to receive God (*Mark 9:37*), to honor Christ is to honor God (*John 5:23*); and to reject Christ is to reject God (*Luke 10:16*). John states that He is the Vine, the source of life. We are the branches, the channels of life. We can bear lasting fruit only if we are drawing life from the Vine, Christ. So, to what extend are you looking to Jesus as the true source of your security, significance, and fulfillment?

When we grow in the Lord, Christ's life is seen by others as we take initiative to witness in the power of the Holy Spirit *(Matthew 28:18-20; Acts 1:8; Colossians 4:2-6)*. Like the first century Christ followers, we have to be sold out for the cause of Christ and transform our world as our lives become living epistles of the Gospel of Grace *(2 Corinthians 3:2)*. *Colossians 4:2-6* teaches us how to learn to become more effective as an instrument of the Holy Spirit to reproduce the life of Christ in others. And as we come to be more like Christ, the Living Stone, we too like living stones are being built into spiritual house *(1 Peter 2:5)*.

I believe God wants each one of us to grow in our understanding that Christ's life and destiny is our life and destiny *(2 Corinthians 4:16-18; Ephesians 1:3; 17-19; 3:16-19; Philippians 1:21; 3:20-21; 1 Peter 1:3-9)*. We have to develop an eternal perspective in the midst of earthly problems. We have to get to where we are able to live above our circumstances. And I believe that can happen when we get the revelation on who we are in Christ and what are future holds. As we learn to set our minds on the Person, the Powers, and the Perfections of God, our will and emotions will come into alignment with His truth, and true wisdom from above *(James 3:17)*. True wisdom is seeing our life from God's view by setting our minds on things above *(Colossians 3:1-3)*. Wisdom is the key to a life of beauty, fulfillment, and purpose *(Proverbs*

3:15-18). Wisdom is the skill in the art of living life with every area under the Lordship of God. It is the ability to use the best means at the best time to accomplish the best results. And God wants us to have His best. This treasure of wisdom is in God's hands and we cannot get it apart from Him *(Proverbs 2:6)*.

Growing spiritually in the Christian life is only successful with the Holy Spirit. It is through Him that we have access to the both God the Father and God the Son *(Ephesians 2:18)*. The Holy Spirit helps us become the kind of person God wants us to become in Him. He is our Teacher and our Guide. He is also our Helper. The Bible teaches us to keep asking, keep seeking, and keep knocking and the heavenly Father will give the Holy Spirit to those who ask Him *(Luke 11:9-13)*. We have to desire to be led by Him. It takes faith to receive the Spirit *(Galatians 3:2; Romans 10:17)*.

Christ comforted the disciples before He had to go to the cross by telling them that another Comforter will come after Him *(John 14:26; 15:26-27; 16:13-14)*. Jesus commanded them to tarry in Jerusalem for the Promise from the Father *(Acts 1:4-5)*. The Holy Spirit was given to empower the Believer for the life which is now in Christ Jesus. "But ye shall receive power, after that the Holy Ghost is come upon you: and ye shall be witnesses unto me both in Jerusalem, and in all Judaea, and in Samaria, and unto the uttermost part of the earth." (Acts 1:8).

The maturity of the Christian depends on being filled with

the Spirit (*Ephesians 5:18*) in order to walk in the Spirit. This filling is crucial to the success of living this new life in Christ. Christians are enabled by the Spirit to manifest Christ-like character. Before the filling of the Spirit, one must yield to Him. Confessing one's sin and being born again is not enough to automatically walk in the Spirit. He or She must yield themselves as an instrument for God's service. *Romans 12:1* and teaches us that we are to present our bodies as living sacrifice unto God. We yield our bodies unto God and our members as members of righteousness unto God (*Romans 6:13; James 4:7*). This yielding both require the body and the mind (*Romans 12:2*). Whatever is conceived in the mind will be carried out with the body. The Christian that relies on their own strengthen to live successfully will fail. But they have to appropriate the power of the Holy Spirit not only day by day, but moment by moment by faith. There has to be a trust that the Holy Spirit will empower them. It is simply relying on the Spirit's help. Our spiritual growth is a result of trusting The Holy Spirit by a life of faith in God.

I believe in order to really and truly begin to grow in the new life in Christ, there has to be a total surrender to God in all that pertains to our lives. God wants to be allowed to work in us according to what pleases Him. He is able to work His work every day and every hour. Therefore, He gives us grace to surrender totally because we cannot do it in our strength, by the power of our will. The Scriptures tells us that "It is God that worketh in us, both to will and to do His good pleasure. When we surrender to God, the Holy Spirit becomes the power in our hearts and life to grow in the grace and knowledge of our Lord (*2 Peter 3:18*).

Second Peter teaches us why we need to grow spiritually in this new life. Growing spiritually is the best solution for error and deception of the Word of God. A mature understanding of the truth lets us know that "According as his divine power hath given unto us all things that pertain unto life and godliness, through the knowledge of him that hath called us to glory and virtue" (*2 Peter 1:3*). Our Christian character is cultivated as we grow. We are reminded that we have been called away from the corruption of the world to conformity with Christ.

Without spiritual growth, a believer will fail to transform profession into practice. We grow in Christ by adding to our faith virtue; and to virtue knowledge; and to knowledge temperance or self-control; and to temperance patience or endurance; and to patience godliness; and to godliness brotherly kindness; and to brotherly kindness charity or love. For when we have these characteristics in increasing measure, they will keep us from being ineffective and unproductive in our knowledge of the Jesus Christ our Lord (*2 Peter 1:5-10*). Growing spiritually is a life-long process as we read, study and apply the Word of God. It is our duty as New Creatures to do our best to present ourselves to God as an approved worker that is not ashamed because we handle the word of truth correctly (*2 Timothy 2:15*). *2 Timothy 3:16-17* teaches us, "All Scripture is God-breathed and is useful for teaching, rebuking, correcting and training in righteousness, so that the man of God may be thoroughly equipped for every good work." In this spiritual growth, we must be taught, rebuked, corrected, and trained by God's Word. Then we will be thoroughly equipped for every good work.

Verses Pertaining to Spiritual Growth to Consider

2 Peter 3:18
"but grow in the grace and knowledge of our Lord and Savior Jesus Christ To Him be the glory, both now and to the day of eternity. Amen."

Ephesians 3:17-19
"so that Christ may dwell in your hearts through faith; and that you, being rooted and grounded in love, may be able to comprehend with all the saints what is the breadth and length and height and depth, and to know the love of Christ which surpasses knowledge, that you may be filled up to all the fullness of God."

1 Peter 2:2
"Like newborn babies, long for the pure milk of the word, so that by it you may grow in respect to salvation,"

Colossians 3:16
"Let the word of Christ richly dwell within you, with all wisdom teaching and admonishing one another with psalms and hymns and spiritual songs, singing with thankfulness in your hearts to God."

1 Timothy 4:15
"Take pains with these things; be absorbed in them, so that your progress will be evident to all."

Ephesians 4:15
"but speaking the truth in love, we are to grow up in all

aspects into Him who is the head, even Christ,"

1 Corinthians 13:11
"When I was a child, I used to speak like a child, think like a child, reason like a child; when I became a man, I did away with childish things."

Colossians 2:6-7
"Therefore as you have received Christ Jesus the Lord, so walk in Him, having been firmly rooted and now being built up in Him and established in your faith, just as you were instructed, and overflowing with gratitude."

Colossians 3:9-10
"Do not lie to one another, since you laid aside the old self with its evil practices, and have put on the new self who is being renewed to a true knowledge according to the image of the One who created him—"

Hebrews 6:1-2
"Therefore leaving the elementary teaching about the Christ, let us press on to maturity, not laying again a foundation of repentance from dead works and of faith toward God, of instruction about washings and laying on of hands, and the resurrection of the dead and eternal judgment."

John 15:5
"I am the vine, you are the branches; he who abides in Me and I in him, he bears much fruit, for apart from Me you can do nothing."

James 1:2-4

"Consider it all joy, my brethren, when you encounter various trials, knowing that the testing of your faith produces endurance. And let endurance have its perfect result, so that you may be perfect and complete, lacking in nothing."

Romans 5:3-4

"And not only this, but we also exult in our tribulations, knowing that tribulation brings about perseverance; and perseverance, proven character; and proven character, hope;"

2 Corinthians 3:18

"But we all, with unveiled face, beholding as in a mirror the glory of the Lord, are being transformed into the same image from glory to glory, just as from the Lord, the Spirit."

New Beginning: The Promise of the Holy Spirit

Chapter Twelve

When a person is born again the Holy Spirit takes up residence. Apostle Paul wrote to the Corinth believers in 1 *Corinthians 3:16*, "Know ye not that ye are a temple of God, and that the Spirit of God dwelleth in you?" The Holy Spirit was given after Jesus ascended back to heaven. "And I will pray the Father, and He shall give you another Comforter, that He may abide with you forever; even the Spirit of Truth, whom the world cannot receive, because it seeth Him not, neither knoweth Him: but ye know Him; for He dwelleth with you and shall be in you (*John 14:16-17*). Those who does not have the Spirit of Christ does not belong to Him (*Romans 8:9)*. As children of God, we need not ask the Holy Spirit to come and live in us. Rather we recognize His presence, His gracious and His glorious indwelling and give Him complete control. The beginning of the new life in Christ is to receive the Holy Spirit.

The indwelling Spirit is a source of full and everlasting satisfaction and successful Christian living. The Holy Spirit completely and forever satisfies the person who allows Him in. We have to realize that we are helpless in living a successful Christian life without the Spirit. The Holy Spirit in Christ Jesus does that which we cannot do for ourselves. We have to surrender our every thought, purpose, desire, and affection to His absolute control. *Galatians 5:16* states that we walk after the Spirit so we won't satisfy the flesh. The life of the Spirit in us must be maintained by the study of the Word and prayer.

It is the Holy Spirit who gives life *(John 6:63)*. In *2 Corinthians 3:6,* we are taught that the letter kills, but Spirit gives life. The Holy Spirit creates the new life. The sinner is born-again by the Spirit. The Holy Spirit is the promise that was sent by God when Jesus ascended back to heaven *(John 15:26)*. The disciples were commanded to remain in Jerusalem until they receive power from the Holy Spirit *(Acts 1:4-8)*. The Holy Spirit was not given to the first-century Believers only. All Believers are indwelt by the Holy Spirit and have power available *(1 Corinthians 6:19)* and must appropriate it by faith daily *(Romans 8:4-5)*.

In the new life in Christ, the Holy Spirit is given to indwell Christians *(1 Corinthians 6:19)*. This is to control the new nature given at conversion *(2 Corinthians 5:17; Ephesians 3:16)*. The Holy Spirit also fills the born-again Believers. Ephesians 5:18 tells us to "be filled with the Spirit". In other words, it is not that the Believer gets more of the Holy Spirit but the Holy Spirit gets more of the Believer. There is a difference between the indwelling of the Holy Spirit and the baptism in the Holy Spirit. The first qualifies us for heaven, but the second equips us for life on earth. The Lord Jesus generously pours out the Holy Spirit on us to equip us with supernatural power to be His witnesses. The Holy Spirit sanctifies the Believer *(Romans 15:16; 2 Thessalonians 2:13)*. The Holy Spirit produces fruit in the life of the Believer *(Galatians 5:22, 23)*. The Holy Spirit imparts gifts to Believers *(Romans 12:6-8); 1*

Corinthians 12:1-11; Ephesians 4:7-12). These gifts are given to glorify God (*Revelation 4:11*) and to edify the Body of Christ (*Ephesians 4:12-13*). Then the Holy Spirit teaches Believers in all spiritual things as we read the Word of God (*John 14:26*) and abide in Christ (*1 John 2:24-27*).

A person may be regenerated by the Holy Spirit and still not be baptized with the Holy Spirit. In regeneration, there is the impartation of life by the Spirit's power and the person who receives it is saved. However, in the baptism with the Holy Spirit, there is the impartation of power, and the person who receives it is fitted for service. *Luke 24:49* states, "And behold I send the promise of My Father upon you: but tarry ye in the city of Jerusalem, until ye be endued with power from on high." And again, in *Acts 1:5* and *8*, "For John truly baptized with water; but ye shall be baptized with the Holy Ghost not many days hence.... But ye shall receive power after that the Holy Ghost is come upon you: and ye shall be witnesses unto Me, both in Jerusalem, and in all Judea, and in Samaria, and unto the uttermost part of the earth. The baptism with the Holy Spirit is not primarily to make believers happy or give them goose bumps or run around the church, but to make them useful and efficient in the Body of Christ. It gives the power to witness for Christ and win others for Christ. I can't overemphasize this important truth enough: The Holy Spirit is absolutely necessary for efficient and effective work for Christ. Even Jesus was baptized by the Spirit. *Acts 10:38*, "How God anointed Jesus of Nazareth with the Holy Ghost and power; who went about doing good, and healing all that were oppressed of the devil; for god was with Him." And also in *Luke 4:1*, "And Jesus, full of the Holy Spirit, returned from the Jordan, and was led by the Sprit in the wilderness."

There is one baptism but many manifestations of the power of the baptism. There are diversities of gifts, but the same Spirit. These gifts vary with the different lines of service to which God calls each of us. The scripture teaches us in 1 *Corinthians 12:4-13*, "Now there are diversities of gifts, but the same Spirit. And there are diversities of gifts, but the same Spirit. And there are differences of administration, but the same Lord. And there are diversities of operations, but it is the same God which worketh all in all. But the manifestation of the Spirit is given too every man to profit withal. For to one is given by the Spirit the word of wisdom; to another the word of knowledge by the same Spirit; to another faith by the same Spirit; to another the gifts of healing by the same Spirit; to another the working of miracles; to another diverse kind of tongues; to another the interpretation of tongues: but all these worketh that one and the selfsame Spirit, dividing to every man severally as He will. For as the body is one, and hath many members, and all the members of that one body, being many, are one body: so also, is Christ. For by one Spirit are we all baptized into one body, whether we be Jews or Gentiles, whether we be bond or free; and have been all made to drink into one Spirit." The manifestation of the Spirit is given to profit the Body (*1 Corinthians 12:7*). And the body grows by that which every joint supply (*Ephesians 4:16*), and to each least significant joint, the Holy Spirit imparts power to perform the function that belongs to him. It is the Holy

Spirit that decides how that is, in what special gift, operation, or power, the baptism shall manifest itself. It is not for us to pick out what field or service we want and then ask Him to qualify us. We just have to surrender to Him and be obedient to Him.

The point I want to make is not about not sinning but living in righteousness. This is impossible with man but possible with God. As Christians, we should not be living a life of living low and failure and sin but a life of rest and victory in Christ by His Spirit.

I will use *Romans 7* to illustrate what I am trying to get across. Here is Paul, a regenerate man, trying in his power to live a holy life. This verse states: "I delight in the law of God after the inward man. To will what is good is present with me. My heart loves the law of God, and my will has chosen that law." Even with a heart full of delight in God's law and with a will determined to do right, it is possible to fail. Why? Because something more is needed. The divine omnipotence is needed to do the work in us. Apostle Paul wrote: It is God which worketh in you, both to will and to do (*Philippians 2:13*). The will can be present to do what is right but we cannot perform it. When God has made us new, God gives us the power to accomplish what that will desires. There are many scriptures that teaches us that the Lord will teach us His ways so that we may walk in His paths *(Isaiah 2:3)*.

It is in humility that we learn that living this new life is impossible for us but all things are possible with God. Our

Christian lives should be proof that God works impossibilities. We can use the virgin Mary. The birth of Jesus was a miracle wrought by the omnipotence of God. Look at the resurrection of our Lord. He was raised by the exceeding greatness of God's mighty power (*Ephesians 1:19-20*). Our new life has its beginning in the omnipotence of God and we must continue in that same power. We have to come to the end of ourselves and totally let God work His will in us. In worship, in work, in sanctification, in obedience to God, we can do nothing in and of ourselves.

It is possible for God to make us surrender and He is able to maintain it. He uses His Word and the Holy Spirit to sanctify us. It is an omnipotent God working by His omnipotence according to His good pleasure. The Bible teaches that the heart is deceitful above all things (*Jeremiah 17:9*), but thanks be to God who has given us a new heart by His power. As new creatures in Christ, we taught to put off our former way of life (*Ephesians 4:22*).

Romans 7:22-25 ends with what is impossible for man. "O wretched man that I am! Who shall deliver me from the body of this death? I thank God through Jesus Christ our Lord." It is humanly impossible to live a righteous life. The born-again believer may be able to serve God in the mind but in the flesh, serve the law of sin. But in Chapter 8, we are taught the nature of God's provision for our deliverance. And it all starts with dependence upon God. In this chapter, the Holy Spirit is the prominent subject. While Chapter 7 focuses on the flesh, chapter 8, the focal point is the Holy Spirit. He is God's provision for holy living in the new life in Christ. He is the answer to the problem of this body of death. Paul is teaching about the ministry of the Holy Spirit that pertains to our salvation and sanctification.

We know that at the time we are born-again, we receive all of the Spirit at the time of salvation. It is not that we need to receive more of the Holy Spirit but whether the Spirit have all of us. Therefore, it is not a matter of having the Him but walking in Him. In our salvation and sanctification, the Holy Spirit initiates, guides, and empowers us so that the righteousness God requires is fulfilled *(8:9-14)*. In the new life, we need not be overcome by guilt or by fear because the Cross of Jesus Christ is the solution. And all who are in Christ by faith there is no condemnation because we walk after the Spirit *(vs. 1)*. Through the prompting of the power of the Spirit, God achieves the righteousness which the Law requires in and through the born-again believer. We must understand that God's work can never be accomplished by our efforts. "Not by might nor by power, but by My Spirit, says the Lord of Hosts" *(Zechariah 4:6)*. God shows us that in the Holy Spirit we have the power of obedience, the power of victory and the power of real holiness *(Romans 8:13)*. Praise the Lord for the Holy Spirit! Often times He is thought to be a luxury or for something special or for certain men and women in ministry. But I have come to learn that the Holy Spirit is necessary for every believer, every moment of the day living in this new life. There is no good in going to church or studying our Bibles and praying if our lives aren't filled with the Holy Spirit.

I will close with this. God gives us the Holy Spirit that we may live every day in the power of the Holy Spirit. And to live a life acceptable to God in the enjoyment of God's salvation and God's love, to live and walk in the power of the new life we must be guided by the Holy Spirit every hour of the day. It is with the power of the Holy Spirit we can live this new life in Christ. There is no secret formula that makes the Spirit's power available. You have to simply rely on His help. Let us surrender to God's will, His ways, and His paths. For those who are in the flesh cannot please God *(Romans 8:8)*.

The Work of the Holy Spirit in Christian Living

The Spirit delivers us from the power of the flesh, gives sonship, assures future glory and assures final victory.

• The Holy Spirit indwells all believers to control the newly created nature given when we are born again (*1 Corinthians 6:19; 2 Corinthians 5:17; Ephesians 3:16*).

• The Holy Spirit fills believers. *Ephesians 5:18* commands us to "be filled with the Spirit". It means to be controlled. Simply put the Holy Spirit gets more of us.

• The Holy Spirit sanctifies the believer. *(Romans 15:16; 2 Thessalonians 2:13)*

• The Holy Spirit produces fruit in the life of the believer. (*Galatians 5:22-23*)

• The Holy Spirit imparts gifts to believers (*Romans 12:6-8; 1 Corinthians 12:1-11; Ephesians 4:7-12*). These gifts are given to glorify God (*Rev. 4:11*) and to edify the body of Christ (*Ephesians 4:13-13*).

• The Holy Spirit teaches believers. *John 14:26* says He will instruct us in all spiritual things as we read the word of God and abide in the son of God (*1 John 2:24-27*)

"And we are his witness of these things; and so is also the Holy Ghost, whom God hath given to them that obey him." *Acts 5:32*

Assurance of Salvation
A Prepared Place for a Prepared People

Chapter Thirteen

Eternal life begins the moment we become born-again. Believers don't have to wait for eternal life because it is not something that happens when we die but it begins when we believe by faith in Christ. *John 3:36* says, "Whoever believes in the Son has eternal life." This is present tense. One of the words commonly used in the New Testament for "eternal" is aiṓnios (ahee-o'-nee-os). It is defined as life operates simultaneously outside of time, inside of time, and beyond time. It does not focus on the future per se but rather on the quality of the age it relates to. Thus, believers live in "eternal life" right now, experiencing this quality of God's life now as a present possession (Strong's Concordance 166). Please note that eternal life is not associated with years but it is independent of time. Eternal life can function outside of and beyond time, as well as within time. Eternal life is the Presence of God. Although we have eternal life now, we are still living on the earth and subject to earthly challenges and hardships, sorrows and disappointments.

In *John 14:2-4*, Jesus told the disciples that He is going to prepare a place for them and will be back to take them to be with Him. Because He goes to prepare a place, He will certainly return for those who have been prepared for the prepared place. The new life in Christ gets us prepared for that place. Christ first coming was to save us and deliver us from the wrath to come *(John 3:17; 1 Thessalonians 1:10)*. This is just a rehearsal. We are practicing for our eternal home with the Lord. We practice heaven on earth. We practice the truth. We practice righteousness. We practice the Presence.

Christ is the Believer's hope of salvation both now and at His coming. Our hope is not only for this present life but we look forward to the time when we will put off our mortal body for our immortal body *(1 Corinthians 15:53)*. All born again Believers have the assurance of salvation, i.e., the certainty that when Jesus comes back or when death comes, he or she will be with the Lord *(Philippians 1:23)*. The return of Christ our Lord is a reassuring and joyful hope for Believers. Because at His coming we will be in the presence of God and will see His face. He will deliver *(1 Thessalonians 1:10; 5:4-11)*, He will reward *(1 Thessalonians 1:19)*, He will perfect *(1 Thessalonians 3:13), He will resurrect (1 Thessalonians 4:13-18), and He* will sanctify *(1 Thessalonians 5:23)* all who are in Christ.

The day of the Lord will come like a thief in the night. But Believers are not in the dark so that day will not catch them off guard *(2 Peter 3:10)*. Believers are children of the Light and the children of the day. Therefore, Believers are to watch and be alert by putting on the breastplate of faith, and love; and for a helmet, the hope of salvation. God has appointed us to obtain salvation by Christ *(1 Thessalonians 5:2-11)*.

In *1 Thessalonians 4:16-17*, Apostle Paul gave revelation concerning the Dead in Christ. It states, "For the Lord himself will come down from heaven with a loud command, with the voice of the archangel and with the trumpet call of God, and the dead in Christ will rise first. After that we who are still alive and are left will be caught up together with them in the clouds to meet the Lord in the air. And so, we will be with the Lord forever." The believers will be transfigured and their bodies will be clothed with immortality (*1 Corinthians 15:51, 53*). It will happen quickly, "in the twinkling of an eye" (*1 Corinthians 15:52*). They will be caught up together to meet Christ in the air. As it is stated we won't all die but will be visibly united with Christ (*1 Thessalonians 4:16-17*).

The hope that our Savior will soon return to take us out of the world to "be with the Lord forever" (*1 Thessalonians 4:17*) is the blessed hope of those in Christ as the redeemed (*Titus 2:13*). We have the hope that we will be saved from the wrath of God as recorded in *Revelation 14:10-11*. We will be saved from the full strength of His indignation from the torment with fire and brimstone. We will be saved from the smoke of torment forever and ever where there will be no rest day and night. And because of the new life in Christ, we give the thanks to the Father who has qualified us to be partakers of the inheritance of the saints of life (*Colossians 1:12*). This is our motivation of future reward: "Wherefore we labour, that, whether present or absent, we may be accepted of him. For we must all appear before the judgment seat of Christ; that every one may receive the things done in his body, according to that he hath done, whether it be good or bad (*2 Corinthians 5:9-10*). So, remember that in everything we do we begin with

God. We have to surrender, give up, and let go. We have to be determined. The bottom line is that heaven is a prepared place for a prepared people.

When we fully understand the end of history, its impact will radically affect the present. The book of Revelation is the Revelation of Jesus Christ (*1:1*). The book begins with a vision of His glory, wisdom and power. It portrays His authority over the entire church. Christ is the Lamb who was slain and declared worthy to open the book of judgment. The Lamb's righteous wrath will be poured out upon the whole earth and He will return in power and judge His enemies and to reign as the Lord over all. This second coming, the King of kings and the Lord of lords will rule forever and ever. As our new life in Christ, we are assured that we have the ultimate triumph of Christ over all who rise up against Him and His saints. This should encourage us to persevere by standing firm in Christ in view of God's plan for the righteous and the wicked. A new universe is created perfect without sin, death, pain, or sorrow (*Revelation 21:4*).

We have an assurance of taking up residence in the new Jerusalem in the very presence of God. The Apostle John sees a river flowing from the "throne of God and the Lamb", and "on each side of the river stood the tree of life" (*Revelation 22:1-2*). We will have restored access to the tree of life. We are assured that Christ is coming quickly. *Revelation 22:12-13* states, "And, behold, I come quickly; and my reward is with me, to give every man according as his work shall be. I am Alpha and Omega, the beginning and the end, the first and the last." May the grace of our Lord Jesus Christ be with all of us. Amen. *(Revelation 22:21).*

Our Goal: Christ Formed in Us

Chapter Fourteen

Apostle Paul described his work in this way: "My dear children, for whom I am again in the pains of childbirth until Christ is formed in you..." (*Galatians 4:19*). Paul's work in the church at Galatia was to help Christ be formed in them by faith and not by works. He worked so that Christ would live in them (*Galatians 2:20*), so that they would be more like Christ. Having Christ formed in them meant that they had the freedom to produce the fruits of righteousness through a Spirit-led life-style.

Thus, our goal is to have Christ be formed in us. We have to allow the Spirit of God to come and shape us from within. He is willing to do this to those who abandon themselves to Him as the Potter. We are transformed by the renewing of our minds — not conformed to this world, but to the pattern of Jesus Christ (*Romans. 12:2*). We are being shaped by the Spirit of Christ into what He wants us to be. He is formed in us by using the gifts He has given each of us, by doing the work He has given us, and by being instruments of righteousness as we submit our lives to Him.

Christ being formed in us does not happen by chance or coincidence. Nor does He force it to happen. Therefore, we must turn to him and seek him by faith. Faith is the assurance that He will do just what He has said and we can rest in the all-sufficiency of what Christ did on the Cross. He that has begun a good work in us will complete it *(Philippians 1:6)*. We have to work out our own salvation with fear and trembling. Why? For it is God who works in us, both to will and to work for His good pleasure *(Philippians 2:12-16)*.

The desire of the new life in Christ is to be like Christ. Therefore, we must know who He is and what He did. We must read and study the Word. We must love Him because He first loved us. We must be humble *(Philippians 2:5)*. We must be obedient. We must be fully dedicated to serving the true God. This service is until we "reach unity in the faith and in the knowledge of the Son of God and become mature, attaining to the whole measure of the fullness of Christ" *(Ephesians 4:13)*.

In this present age, we will not be able to fully reach this goal that is Christ but it is a continuing process. Therefore, we will run this race with patience that is set before us *(Hebrews 12:1)*. Because we have the promise that if we continue faithfully, a crown of righteousness is assured for us *(2 Timothy 4:8)*. Know that we "are being transformed into his likeness with ever-increasing glory" *(2 Corinthians 3:18)*.

Thanks be to God that we are already being transformed into the likeness of Christ. For isn't that what salvation is all about: We give our lives to Him on a daily basis, and He shapes us to become more like Him. God saved us, is saving us and will save us for this very reason: that we become like His Son. This process starts when we have taken off our old self with its practices and have put on the new self, which is being renewed in knowledge in the image of its Creator (*Colossians 3:9-10*)." *Ephesians 4:22-24* states it this way: "Put off your old self, which is being corrupted by its deceitful desires; to be made new in the attitude of your minds, and to put on the new self, created to be like God in true righteousness and holiness." Out with the old, and in with the new! Put off wrong ways, and put on the way of Christ. It begins from the inside and is manifested on the outside.

We have to be committed to a lifelong process day by day. Jesus said in *Matthew 16:24*, "If anyone would come after me, let him deny himself take up his cross and follow me. This means that we are willing to die in order to follow Jesus. We make the decision to surrender to His will. As Christ is formed in us, we experience our true identity in Christ. When our life is centered on Jesus as well as in Jesus, who not only shows us the Father, he also shows us who we are in Him.

The new life in Christ has a great responsibility. As disciples of Christ, we are commissioned also as Jesus told his disciples, "Go and make disciples of all nations, baptizing them in the name of the Father and of the Son and of the Holy Spirit, and teaching them to obey everything I have commanded you" (*Matthew 28:19-20*). As His disciples, we are to teach the things He taught, to do the things He said to do, to believe the things He said to believe.

We have the confidence that of Lord and Savior will not abandon us. He said that He will never leave us or forsake us (*Hebrews 13:5*). The ultimate supreme sacrifice was done when

He sent His Only Son to die for us; we can be assured that God will not forget what He is doing in our lives. God, our Father is shaping us, changing us, and transforming us to be more and more like Jesus Christ. We are His heirs and we are being created anew through the Holy Spirit. And our destiny is for glory and to be like Christ eternally!

Therefore, my brothers and sisters in Christ Jesus, let Christ be formed in us, and labor so that He may be formed in all the church. Let us follow the example of Jesus and be about our Father's business, seeking His will, seeking Him. Let Him change us for His purpose, and our glory will be his glory (*Luke 2:49; John 4:34; John 6:38; John 5:30; Matthew 6:10*).

May the God of Grace Jesus see us through as we seek to do the work He has called and chosen us to do. Amen!

Epilogue

Chapter Fifteen

New Life in Christ by Faith:

1. We receive eternal life. *~John 3:16*
2. We are given salvation as a gift, not by works, so no one can boast because Jesus did the work. *~Ephesians 2:8*
3. We receive forgiveness of sin; we are justified. *~Romans 5:9*
4. We receive Christ's own righteousness because our righteousness is as filthy rags. *~2 Corinthians 5:21; Philippians 3:9*
5. We receive a new nature. *~Ephesians 4:24*
6. We become one with Christ's death, burial, and resurrection. *~Romans 6:3-5*
7. We are no longer slaves to sin. *~Romans 6:6*
8. Sin no longer has dominion over us (we may feel like we need to sin, but we don't have to). *~Romans 6:6*
9. We become a disciple:
a. The work begins – discipleship costs. *~Luke 14:25*
b. Turn from sin, and turn to God. *~Acts 3:19*
c. Put sin to death. *~Colossians 3:5; Romans 8:11-13*
d. Learn to obey what God says. *~Romans 1:5; John 14:15; 2 John 1:6; Revelation 14:12*
e. Deny yourself, take up your cross, and follow Jesus daily (moment by moment). *~Luke 9:23-24*

In Christ, we have all the power and resources we need to live a life of victory. "All power and authority has been given to Me in heaven and earth" (*Matthew 28:18*), and aren't we joint-heir with Him? When we lack the knowledge, or choose to be ignorant of this, we will continue to practice sin. We will continue to make excuses like: "we are only human;" "we sin every day;" and "no one is perfect." But the Bible teaches me that I no longer have to present the members of my body to sin as instruments of unrighteousness because I have new life and new power in Christ. I can successfully stop sowing to the flesh and sow to the Spirit *(Roman 6)*. All we have to do is believe God's word. Should we put more faith in Adam's offense where death reigns than in the abundance of grace and the gift of righteousness where we can reign in life through Christ? Absolutely NOT! "For if by the one man's offense death reigned through the one, much more those who receive abundance of grace and of the gift of righteousness will reign in life through the One, Jesus Christ" (*Romans 5:17 NKJV*).

Will you sow to the flesh or to the Spirit? When we sow to the flesh, we reap corruption. When we sow to the Spirit, we reap everlasting life (*Galatians 6:7-8*). As we make the choice that the world has been crucified to us and we to the world as a new creation (*Galatians 6:15*), we will have crucified the flesh with its passions and desires (*Galatians 5:24*). The results will bear the fruit of the Spirit (*Galatians 5:22*).

Although this is a sanctifying work by the Word of God and the Holy Spirit, I believe we can indeed be delivered and set free from habitually sinning. No longer do we have to be slaves to sin, for we can draw near to the throne of grace for help in time of need (*Hebrews 4:11*). He always gives us a way of escape *(1 Corinthians 10:13)*. We can continuously be changed inwardly and be able to live a righteous life outwardly by the power of the Holy Spirit and God's Word. I believe this is working out our salvation (*Philippians 2:12*). Simply put, it is the salvation that Jesus Christ has already accomplished for us that should manifested in how we live.

The same grace that saves us from sin is the same grace that will keep us from sin. "You have accepted Jesus as your Lord; keep on following Him. Plant your roots in Christ and let Him be the Foundation for your life. Be strong in your faith" (*Colossians 2:6*) and don't frustrate the grace of God (*Galatians 2:21*). Everything that God has for us is appropriated in Christ. "All the promises of God are Yes and Amen in Christ (*2 Corinthians 1:20*). Our spiritual life is lived in Christ; therefore, "let our conduct be worthy of the gospel of Christ" *(Philippians 1:27)*.

May the God of peace equip us with everything good for doing His will, and may He work in us what is pleasing to Him through Jesus Christ to whom be glory forever and ever. Amen. (*Hebrews 13:20*)

In God's Hands for His Glory,
Mary J. Bryant

How to Experience New Life in Christ Jesus

• Everyone is a sinner and is separated from God "For all have sinned, and come short of the glory of God" ~*Romans 3:23*

• God loved us all so much that He gave his Son to be punished and die for our sin. "But God commendeth his love toward us, in that, while we were yet sinners, Christ died for us" ~*Romans 5:8*

• Death means separation forever from God. Eternal life comes by trusting Jesus Christ. "For the wages of sin is death, but the gift of God is eternal life through Jesus Christ our Lord" ~*Romans 6:23*

• In order to begin your new life in Christ (be saved), you must believe that you are a sinner and that Jesus was punished and died for your sins; repent and turn to God believing in Jesus and accept the salvation of your soul. "If thou shalt confess with thy mouth the Lord Jesus and shalt believe in thine heart that God hath raised him from the dead, thou shalt be saved" ~*Romans 10:9*

• This is God's promise to you if you accept Jesus, He will accept you. "For whosoever shall call upon the name of the Lord shall be saved" ~*Romans 10:13*

• If you would like to accept Jesus now, pray a similar prayer: "Dear God, I know I have sinned and I want to receive the forgiveness that Jesus paid for on the cross. I repent from my ways and turn to your way. I now accept your offer of eternal life. I will follow Jesus as my Savior and Lord and will obey Him in all that I do. Thank You Lord for my new life.

• Now use your faith to walk this new life out by the aid of the Holy Spirit.

Grace and Peace in Abundance,
Mary J. Bryant

"Therefore judge nothing before the appointed time; wait until the Lord comes. He will bring to light what is hidden in darkness and will expose the motives of the heart. At that time each will receive their praise from God."

1 Corinthians 4:5 NIV

ABOUT THE AUTHOR

In writing as an inspirational author, I am aware that I can only be effective and fruitful as soul winners to the lost and encouragers to the saints of God as I am filled with the Holy Spirit and totally and exclusively rely on the power of God's Word. My greatest testimony of the gospel of salvation is that I have been transformed by the gospel of Jesus Christ. Thus, my witness is not something I do but it is who I am.

The Gospel is my measuring rod of God's grace (*Titus 2:11,15*). Therefore, I must grow in understanding the doctrine of the Gospel. I understand what Apostle Paul meant in *1st Corinthians 2:2* when he said that he wanted to know Christ and Him crucified. The Gospel is the power of God unto salvation and unto sanctification.

I truly believe that the overall approach to present the gospel of Jesus Christ that produces true converts, regenerated people, is to let people know that Jesus Christ willingly died for our sins (*Romans 5:8*). He was buried. He was raised by God from the dead. It has to be emphasized that the gospel of Jesus Christ is the only means of salvation. Through the demonstration of His grace and justice, God gave His Only Son to be our substitute. Literally. Jesus bore the judgment of God on our behalf. God judged Him instead of judging us.

The gospel has to be presented as God's Holy character which demands justice for our sin of unbelief. I understand that unbelief is not saying there is no God, but it is purposefully and willfully rejecting God's plan of salvation through His Son. I once read that unbelief is a state of mind that states they don't need nor want God. In other words, I don't need salvation. Those who are truly born-again and who will be born again, has the revelation that they see themselves as an offense towards God that has separated them from God. And that Jesus Christ is the Only solution or defense against it. Then the Holy Spirit will bring conviction of the sinful condition and the direr consequences of eternal torment being separated from God. It is then one can repent and turn to God for salvation.

With all this in mind, I carefully and prayerfully seek to share this good news so that it can be perceived as foundational in what is offered by God and what is at stake. I believe the good news of Jesus message has to be given as an ultimatum not as an alternative (*John 3:17*) because there is no other name under the heavens where as men can be saved except the name of Jesus (*Acts 4:12*).

"My meat is to do the will of Him that sent me, and to accomplish His work." (*John 4:34*) I seek not my own will, but will of Him that sent me." (*John 5:30; see 6:38*) – preach/teach the Good News of Grace, edify the saints, lead the lost to the Cross and glorify God.

www.doveministry378.org
Faith in Action YouTube Show

Mary J. Bryant

www.ingramcontent.com/pod-product-compliance
Lightning Source LLC
Chambersburg PA
CBHW031424290426
44110CB00011B/519